Howard and Shirley have written a series of clever, concise, and insightful devotions that provide practical applications of biblical truth to our daily lives. They examine what the Bible says and challenge their readers to interact with Scripture in developing a personal plan of action for spiritual growth and maturity. Their devotions are laced with personal stories, practical applications, and provocative challenges. Don't miss them!

— Ed Hindson, DMin, ThD, DPhil
    Founding Dean, Distinguished Professor of Religion
    Rawlings School of Divinity, Liberty University

Always a challenge—finding just the right devotional for disciples or counselees as they graduate. Of course, you will be finding refreshment for yourself as well!

— Virginia Stewart, PhD
    HOPE Ministries, Christ Presbyterian Church
    Nashville, Tennessee

This devotional offers insightful and meaningful exercises.

— Jeff Forrey, PhD
    Resource Director for Biblical Counseling Coalition
    Adjunct Faculty at Westminster Theological Seminary & Reformed Theological Seminary-Charlotte

These devotionals are well written, interesting, and clear. They are theologically and biblically rich with the right number of stories to help the readers see how truth works in everyday live.

— Howard Dial, ThM, MDiv
    Pastor Emeritus Berach Bible Church
    Fayetteville, Georgia

God wants us to grow in our love for and knowledge of Him. This very practical devotional gives not only a series of wonderful thoughts about God but a plan for growth as a Christian and growth in the love of the Father. As the reader applies these truths he or she will join the Apostle in crying out, "Abba, Father" with a commitment and joy that presses you on to, *lay hold of that for which Christ Jesus laid hold of* [you] (Philippians 3:12).

— Bill Hines, DMin
  President, Covenant Ministries
  Fort Worth, Texas

The devotional at the beginning was clear and convincing. I really like the format. The exercises at the end of each chapter will be very beneficial by encouraging the reader to biblically journal. There is a good variety of themes that assist the reader in applying the Word to his or her life, heart, and circumstances.

— Ken Jones, DMin
  Pastor for Shepherding
  Oak Mountain Presbyterian Church
    Birmingham, Alabama

I appreciate the biblical nature and examples provided, and I like the way the authors have set up the chart-type answer boxes at the end of each chapter so the reader can apply the lesson.

— Sue Nicewander
  Biblical Counseling Ministries
  Wisconsin Rapids, Wisconsin

Feb 2018

To Jodi —

A very helpful, caring administrative gal. I appreciate all you do to make BCC work. As so often is the case, you make the leadership look good. Trust the Lord blesses you working over it all.

Ps 105:1-7

Hope for New Beginnings

Dr. Howard Eyrich
Shirley Crowder

Hope for New Beginnings
© 2017 Shirley Crowder and Howard Eyrich

ISBN-13: 978-0-692961-09-4
ISBN-10: 0-692961-09-7

Unless otherwise noted, all scriptures are taken from *The Holy Bible, New International Version®*, copyright © 1973, 1978, 1984, 2011 by Biblical, Inc.™ Used by permission of Zondervan. All rights reserved worldwide. www.zondervan.com.

Scripture marked "ESV" are from *The Holy Bible, English Standard Version®*, copyright © 2001 by Crossway, 2011 Text Edition. Used by permission. All rights reserved.

Scripture marked "KJV" are from *The Holy Bible, Authorized (King James) Version.*

Scripture marked "NASB" are from *The Holy Bible, New American Standard Bible®*, copyright © 1960, 1962, 1963, 1968, 1971, 1972, 1973, 1975, 1977, 1995 by the Lockman Foundation.

Scripture marked "NKJV" are from *The Holy Bible, New King James Version®*, copyright © 1982 by Thomas Nelson Publishers, Nashville. Used by permission. All rights reserved.

Cover photograph: "Sunrise in Miango, Nigeria" 2017, D'Anna Shotts

Published by Growth Advantage Communications
3867 James Hill Circle
Hoover, Alabama 35226

Dedication

We dedicate this book to Pamela Jayne Eyrich,
beloved wife, mother, grandmother, great-grandmother,
disciple-maker, ministry partner, and friend.

Charm is deceptive, and beauty is fleeting;
but a woman who fears the LORD is to be praised.
Honor her for all that her hands have done,
and let her works bring her praise at the city gate.
Proverbs 31:30-31

Table of Contents

Introduction

While it is exciting to anticipate the adventure, stepping into new beginnings can be unsettling. We might be thrust into situations that tempt us to trust our own desires and follow our emotions.

As Christ-followers, we know that we do not move forward in our own strength, but in the strength of our Savior and Lord Jesus Christ. We understand the Bible is the final authority on every issue. God's Word, the Bible, outweighs our own and anyone else's opinion. In 2 Timothy 3:16-17 we are reminded that *All Scripture is God-breathed and is useful for teaching, rebuking, correcting and training in righteousness; so that the servant of God may be thoroughly equipped for every good work.*

If we understand that God's declaration is what matters, then our desire is to obey His Word, as Psalm 119:11 says, *I have hidden your word in my heart that I might not sin against you.*

We pray that your prayerful consideration of the biblical truths in each devotional and interaction with the Holy Spirit will help steer your thoughts throughout the day as they help you *set your mind on things above* (Colossians 3:2) and not on the things of earth. As you work through the Scripture passages, devotions, and journaling interactions, you will focus on what the Holy Spirit is teaching you and your heart will be transformed, and you will not get bogged down with circumstances surrounding you. As each devotion builds on your knowledge and understanding of Scripture, you will be strengthened to obey God's Word and find delight in Him, and you will be able to step confidently into any new beginning.

You may come across a Scripture passage or something in a devotion that is unfamiliar or that you need to study further. Consult a study Bible or commentary to delve deeper into the biblical truths presented in the devotional.

Good idea

Biblical counselors, when you are ready to dismiss a counselee, this devotional makes a great assignment for the next thirty-one days, then have the counselee come back for a final check-up.

Getting the Most From This Devotional

You may use this as a Daily Devotional or a Weekly Devotional by following the "Individual Devotions" suggestions.

You may choose to work through the devotional with a friend or a group of friends by following the "Devotions with Friends" suggestions.

INDIVIDUAL DEVOTIONS

As a Daily Devotional

Each day, for 31 days, focus on one devotion that will guide you through the following process:

➢ **Pray** Asking the Lord to open your heart to understand the biblical truths presented and for the Holy Spirit to prompt you to repent of any sin He brings to your attention.

➢ **Read the Background Passage** Lays the scriptural foundation for the day's devotion.

➢ **Scripture Observations** Gives space for you to write your observations, key truths, and questions about the Scripture passage.

➢ **Focus on Scripture** Helps you focus in on truths upon which the day's devotion is based.

➢ **Contemplate the Devotion** Guides your thoughts toward the biblical truths contained in the background and focal passages.

➢ **Prayer** Leads you to ask the Lord to enable you to know Him better and to obey His Word as presented in the day's devotion.

➤ **Interact with Biblical Truths** Leads you to a deeper understanding of biblical truths for each devotion. Complete at least one of the interactions each day using the space provided or a separate journal or notebook to write your answers.

➤ **Notes, Thoughts, & Questions** Gives space for you to make notes, record thoughts about the biblical truths in the devotional, and note any questions needing additional study and research.

As a Weekly Devotional

For five days of a week, for 31 weeks, focus on one devotion for that week. This will enable you to spend more time absorbing the depth and meaning of the Scripture and devotion, and to carefully work through all the "Interact with Biblical Truths" exercises. Follow the suggested process, or, create a process that works well for you.

1st Day of Week (CHOOSE ANY DAY TO BEGIN)

➤ **Pray** Asking the Lord to open your heart to understand the biblical truths presented and for the Holy Spirit to prompt you to repent of any sin He brings to your attention.

➤ **Read Background Passage** Lays the scriptural foundation for the day's devotion. Read the passage in at least three different versions of the Bible. You will find many online sources for these. Make note of any key words or phrases.

➤ **Scripture Observations** Gives space for you to write your observations, key truths, and questions about the Scripture passage.

➤ **Focus on Scripture** Helps you focus in truths upon which the day's devotion is based. Write the Scripture on a notecard and put it where you will see it several times each day.

➤ **Prayer** Leads you to ask the Lord to enable you to know Him better and to obey His Word as presented in the day's devotion.

➤ **Notes, Thoughts, and Questions** Gives space for you to make notes, record thoughts about the biblical truths, and note any questions needing additional study and research.

2nd Day of Week

➤ **Pray**

➤ **Read Background Passage** As you read, be sure to note the cross-references in your Bible and any notes that pertain to that passage.

➤ **Scripture Observations** Add any new observations, key truths, and questions about the Scripture passage.

➤ **Focus on Scripture**

➤ **Contemplate the Devotion** As you read the devotion, mark key words or key phrases that stand out to you. Make notes of any other Scripture passages or biblical truths that come to mind.

- ➤ **Prayer**

- ➤ **Notes, Thoughts, and Questions**

3rd Day of Week

- ➤ **Pray**

- ➤ **Read Background Passage**

- ➤ **Scripture Observations** Add any new observations, key truths, and questions about the Scripture passage.

- ➤ **Interact with Biblical Truths** Complete the first interaction exercise.

- ➤ **Prayer**

- ➤ **Notes, Thoughts, and Questions**

4th Day of Week

- ➤ **Pray**

- ➤ **Read Background Passage**

- ➤ **Scripture Observations** Add any new observations, key truths, and questions about the Scripture passage.

- ➤ **Interact with Biblical Truths** Complete the second interaction exercise.

- ➤ **Prayer**

- ➤ **Notes, Thoughts, and Questions**

5th Day of Week

- ➤ **Pray**

➢ **Read Background Passage**

➢ **Scripture Observations** Add any new observations, key truths, and questions about the Scripture passage.

➢ **Interact with Biblical Truths** Complete the third interaction exercise.

➢ **Prayer**

➢ **Notes, Thoughts, and Questions**

DEVOTIONS WITH FRIENDS

Devotion with Friends Leader

If you and one friend are working through the devotional together, take turns leading the discussion. Each of you will follow the Individual Devotions suggestions separately, and the facilitator will follow these suggestions.

If a group of friends is working through the devotional together, you need to determine who will lead each week. The same person may facilitate the discussion each week, or you may rotate. The important point is that someone needs to be responsible to lead the discussion. Each person in the friends group will follow the Individual Devotions suggestions throughout the week. Once the facilitator has completed the devotional, he or she will follow these suggestions to facilitate the discussion.

➢ **Pray** Asking the Lord to open your heart to understand the biblical truths presented and for the Holy Spirit to prompt you to repent of any sin He brings to your attention.

15

➢ **Prepare** Allows time for reading, studying, contemplating, and meditating upon the biblical truths found in each devotion will enable you to lead the discussion. Make sure you complete all of the exercises so that you can help with any questions or discussion on them.

➢ **Facilitate Discussion** Facilitates the flow of the discussion as you consider the Scripture passages, contemplate the devotion, and interact with the biblical truths presented in the devotion.

➢ **Encourage Friends** Enable facilitator to encourage your friends using the biblical truths presented in the Scripture passages and devotion. Also, encourage your friends to complete the reading and interact with biblical truth exercises each week.

As a Daily Devotional Discussion

Each day, for 31 days, focus on one devotion by following the suggestions for Individual Devotions. Set aside a specific time each day to discuss that day's devotional with your friend.

➢ **Pray** Asks the Lord to open your heart to understand the biblical truths presented and for the Holy Spirit to prompt you to repent of any sin He brings to your attention.

➢ **Read the Background Passage** Lays the scriptural foundation for the day's devotion. You may choose any Bible version from which to read.

➢ **Scripture Observations** Allows time for the group to share observations, key truths, and questions about the Scripture.

➢ **Focus on Scripture** Helps the group focus in on truths upon which the day's devotion is based. Facilitator may ask someone who memorized the passage to recite it.

➢ **Contemplate the Devotion** Guides your thoughts toward the biblical truths contained in the background and focal passages. Before reading the devotional, have different group members look up the Scripture passages that are found within the devotional. When you get to that part in the devotional, ask that person to read the Scripture passage. Then continue reading the devotional.

➢ **Prayer** Leads you to ask the Lord to enable you to know Him better and to obey His Word as presented in the day's devotion. Facilitator will pray or ask someone to pray. The prayer may be an impromptu prayer or the suggested prayer that is included in the devotional.

➢ **Interact with Biblical Truths** Leads you to a deeper understanding of biblical truths for each devotion. The Facilitator will lead the group to share their answers. Be sure to read aloud any Scripture passages that are given with each exercise. Remember, the idea is to interact with the biblical truths presented in that day's devotional.

> **Notes, Thoughts, & Questions** Gives opportunity for friends to share their notes, thoughts, and questions.

> **Ending Prayer** Asks the Lord to continue teaching this group of friends through His Holy Spirit-inspired Word.

As a Weekly Devotional Discussion

For five days of a week, for 31 weeks, the Facilitator will focus on one devotion for that week by following the suggestions for Individual Devotions. Set aside a specific time each week to discuss that day's devotional with your friend.

> **Pray** Asks the Lord to open your heart to understand the biblical truths presented and for the Holy Spirit to prompt you to repent of any sin He brings to your attention.

> **Read the Background Passage** Lays the scriptural foundation for the day's devotion. You may choose any Bible version from which to read.

> **Scripture Observations** Allows time for the group to share their observations, key truths, and questions about the Scripture passage.

> **Focus on Scripture** Helps the group focus in on truths upon which the day's devotion is based. Facilitator may ask someone who memorized the passage to recite it.

> **Contemplate the Devotion** Guides your thoughts toward the biblical truths contained in the background and focal passages. Before reading the devotional, have different group members

look up the Scripture passages that are found within the devotional. When you get to that part in the devotional, ask that person to read the Scripture passage. Then continue reading the devotional.

➣ **Prayer** Leads you to ask the Lord to enable you to know Him better and to obey His Word as presented in the day's devotion. Facilitator will pray or ask someone to pray. The prayer may be an impromptu prayer or the suggested prayer that is included in the devotional.

➣ **Interact with Biblical Truths** Leads you to a deeper understanding of biblical truths for each devotion. The Facilitator will lead the group to share their answers. Be sure to read aloud any Scripture passages that are given with each exercise. Remember, the idea is to interact with the biblical truths presented in that day's devotional.

➣ **Notes, Thoughts, & Questions** Gives opportunity for friends to share their notes, thoughts, and questions.

➣ **Ending Prayer** Asks the Lord to continue teaching this group of friends through His Holy Spirit-inspired Word.

Keep yourselves in God's love
READ: Jude 20-22

Scripture Observations

We are beloved of God but it takes effort/intentionality to remain spiritually healthy - connected to God.

Keep yourselves in the love of God,
waiting for the mercy
of our Lord Jesus Christ that leads to eternal life.
Jude 21 (ESV)

Contemplate the Devotion

While on an extended ministry trip throughout the North Island of New Zealand we were privileged to be house guests of several families. One of those households was that of a retired businessman who had spent a lifetime as a self-employed Christian entrepreneur. In this context, he asked me, "As an academic, pastor, and counselor you have lived a full and busy life. Tell me, have you had a separate segment of the day for your walk with the Lord?"

In response, I told him of the rather stringent training I had in seminary regarding this issue. We were instructed to always keep separate our devotional time and our study/preparation time for preaching and teaching. I followed this with an explanation as to why that thinking never made either theological or practical sense to me.

While not drawing upon this particular text from Jude in the conversation, it certainly reflects in part my answer. This was the delineation of my objection to such separation of devotions and study for preaching and teaching. A common theme of the New Testament is walking in worship. Jesus developed this in detail in the Upper Room Discourse in John 14-17. In John 15, He calls us to abide in Him and to demonstrate love for Him through obedience.[1] Obedience is worship. All of life is to be worship. As Martin Luther noted, the most menial functions and tasks in life should be done for the glory of God, and in doing so one lives obediently and worshipfully.

Note the exhortation of our passage for today. The subjects of the exhortation are all believers (Jude 1). Certain imperatives are delineated as believers are told to *build yourselves up in your most holy faith*—engage in studying the Word of God. Be engaged in *praying in the Holy Spirit*—no time categories or limitations; pray always. *Keep yourselves in the love of God*—sounds like Jesus in John 15 when He speaks of abiding in Him by obediently keeping His commandments. *Looking for the mercy of our Lord Jesus*—anticipating that when we see Him we shall be as He is (1 John 3:2).

---

[1] Τηρήσετε—This is a future indicative active verb; therefore he said, "You will be keeping my commandments." Obedience, in this case, is acknowledgement that He is Lord and is therefore worship. Hence, all of life is worship.

Now, is all this a way of saying that we should not have a specific time set aside to engage in focused meditation and prayer? Of course not! But it is saying that getting your ticket punched, so to speak, by having a twenty-minute devotional time is insufficient. Quiet time, outside the context of worshipful living, will likely only salve one's conscience.

So, why *this* devotional, if there is no separate devotional act at a designated time? Good question! Our intent is to put some seasoning on your worshipful day. We hope to encourage you to fulfill all the imperatives of today's text. As you go through the rest of this day, abide in Christ so that your life will look like the life depicted in Psalm 15. We hope that these devotionals will lead to a new beginning for your worshipful living.

Prayer

Father, today I desire to walk in obedience so that all of my life may be a sweet-smelling aroma of worship before You. May others see Jesus in the way I live. May others be encouraged to walk in obedience because I have so lived before the watching world. You said that people will know we belong to You when we love one another, so Father, help me be obedient to love the unlovely brother or sister. When I fail, convict me and help me rush to the cross for fresh cleansing in the blood of Jesus, in whose Name I pray. Amen.

Interact with Biblical Truths (COMPLETE AT LEAST ONE EACH DAY)

➢ In Psalm 15, the psalmist says that *He who does these things will never be shaken*. List *these things* a Christ-follower is to do in order to *never be shaken*, and then honestly rate yourself for how you are doing on each.

Things to do	How I rate (0 to 5) 0-not doing at all 5-do it consistently
1. Walk Blamelessy doing what is right	4
2. Speak truth in his heart	4
3. does not slander	4
4. does no evil to his neighbor	5
5. does not take up a reproach against a friend	4
6. despise vile people & honor those who fear the Lord.	4
7. swears to his own hurt + does not change.	Not sure what this means.
8. Handles money wisely.	3
9.	
10.	
11.	

> Ask forgiveness for the things you just listed that you are not doing well. Beside the corresponding number, write a plan to incorporate these things into your life.

My plan to incorporate them in my life
1. Awareness
2.
3.
4.
5.
6.
7.
8. Curb spending
9.
10.
11.

➢ Name at least two specific ways you are being intentional to experience a worshipful day.

Doing this devotion

Bible in a year plan

Precepts study

Notes, Thoughts, and Questions

God is too loving to be unkind
and too wise to make a mistake.

~Laura Longenecker~
Wife, mother, youth co-leader with husband, Jim

Devo 2
Howard

Let me hear
READ: Psalm 143:8-11

Scripture Observations

_____

_____

_____

_____

Let the morning bring me word of your unfailing love,
for I have put my trust in you.
Show me the way I should go,
for to you I entrust my life.
Psalm 143:8

Contemplate the Devotion

What a wonderful way to set the tone for the day!

The psalmist begins by preparing his heart to receive affirmation from the Lord. We can certainly learn from him. All too often our days begin by tuning our hearts to our favorite news station. When I was a child in school, some seventy years ago, my fourth-grade teacher emphasized the importance of listening to the news on the radio before coming to school. No doubt living through the uncertainty of six years of World War II had ingrained this habit in my teacher. In today's world, the media moguls have captured the beginning of the day—some more liberal or some more conservative newsfeeds and social media—all of which interfere with tuning our hearts to God. As we never know what the day will hold, hearing an affirmation from the Lord of His steadfast love keeps the airbag circuits connected so we are prepared for the crashes of life.

Some years ago, friends heard the phone ringing around ten o'clock in the morning. The mom answered it. A police officer informed her that her bright young daughter, a recent college graduate, was being life-flighted to the hospital after a freak auto accident. My friends are strong Christians who begin their days tuning their hearts to receive the affirmation of the Lord's steadfast love. They were prepared for the crisis.

The Lord's love is steadfast. That simply means that it is love that does not wax and wane. It is dependable! Like the psalmist, we find this love by trusting in God. Trust is resting. This reminds me of the words of Jesus when he said, *Come to me, all you who are weary and burdened, and I will give you rest* (Matthew 11:28). From this place of trust the psalmist utters a second request: *Show me the way I should go.*

When we hear the Lord's affirmation of His steadfast love, it gives us confidence that the best possible pathway for the day is to trust God regardless of what may ensue, because it comes from the Lord who loves with a steadfast love. We can paraphrase the psalmist's closing thought this way, "I place my soul in your hands."

Prayer

Father, through these moments of meditation we join the psalmist in tuning our hearts to hear afresh from You the affirmation of Your steadfast love. We rest our lives in Your merciful goodness and thereby will be prepared to face the uncertainties of living in this fallen world. Because we commit ourselves to walk in the way that You lead, we are able to rejoice always and glorify You. Thank You for Your steadfast love. Amen.

Interact with Biblical Truths (COMPLETE AT LEAST ONE EACH DAY)

➤ List three of your major morning routines that usually set the tone for your day. How do these routines hinder you from receiving affirmation from the Lord? How do these routines prepare you to receive affirmation from the Lord?

Morning Routines	They HINDER or They PREPARE

➢ For the morning routines that hinder you from receiving affirmation from the Lord, write a change you can make so it prepares you to receive that affirmation. If you need new routines, write a plan to begin ones that prepare you to receive affirmation from the Lord.

Change to my routine / New routine to start

➢ Reread Psalm 143:8-11, making note of key words or phrases from these verses. Write the biblical principle the key words or phrases represent.

Key words / Phrases	Biblical Principle

Notes, Thoughts, and Questions

If our principal treasure be as we profess,

in things spiritual and heavenly,

—and woe unto us if it be not so!—

on them will our affections,

and consequently our desires and thoughts,

be principally fixed.

~John Owen~
English Theologian and Pastor

In the beginning God
READ: Genesis 1:1-5

Scripture Observations

_____

_____

_____

_____

In the beginning God created the heavens and the earth.
Genesis 1:1

Contemplate the Devotion

New beginnings are a regular part of life. Sometimes they are well planned, and we eagerly anticipate the future. At other times, we are reticent to move forward into the new beginning. As we think about new beginnings it is appropriate for us to look at the beginning of God's Word—the Bible.

Today's focal passage is the first verse in the first book of the Bible. Here, God is the subject, as He is the subject of the entire Bible. From this verse we learn something very important about God—He existed before the universe was created. God has always been, is now, and will always be, present.

Next, we learn that from nothing God created the universe and everything within it. He is the holy, sovereign, majestic, powerful, all-knowing God.

Every time I read these first few verses of the Bible I am amazed that with just four little words, *Let there be light* (verse 3), the Creator God spoke into existence light that drove away the darkness. What astounding power! From these verses, we learn that God is the Author of light. Other places in Scripture tell us that God is light itself (1 John 1:5), and James calls Him *the Father of lights* (James 1:17).

Think about it: here we are today, many years since God spoke those four little words, *Let there be light,* and as John tells us, *The light shines in the darkness, and the darkness has not overcome it* (John 1:5). The Light—God—brings clarity, order, and understanding, while darkness is seen as evil, void, and chaotic.

I watched the coverage of a solar eclipse on several websites. It was so interesting to listen as a myriad of scientists and others explained the wonders of the universe, and while the science behind it all was quite interesting to me, the coverage fell flat. Why? Because it was totally devoid of any mention of Creator God. Only one man explained the solar eclipse through the lens of God's Word. As he explained the science behind the solar eclipse, he also explained that THE God of the Universe who created everything that we see, holds the entire universe in His hands, and controls everything that happens, including a solar eclipse.

In the midst of a new beginning or anything else going on in your life, the truths in these passages are wonderful reminders that we can step confidently into any new beginning as we trust in the

God who was here *in the beginning*, is here with us now, and who will be with us always. And what a comfort it is to remember that the light of God dispels the darkness and chaos of sin.

Prayer

Heavenly Father, it is sometimes daunting to step into new beginnings, whether it is a new year, a new job, a new relationship, a new home, a new city, or anything else. Help me know you better as I read and study Your Word. Strengthen me to step confidently into the new beginnings in my life. In the Name of Jesus, Amen.

Interact with Biblical Truths (COMPLETE AT LEAST ONE EACH DAY)

➢ Briefly describe a situation when the Light—God—brought clarity, order, and understanding into a situation in your life.

_____

_____

_____

_____

➢ List ways in which knowing THE God of the Universe affects the way you view things like a solar eclipse, a tornado, a drought, etc.

_____

_____

_____

➢ Reread Genesis 1:1-5. Note key words and/or phrases that describe God. How do these aspects of God's character help you trust Him?

Key words / Phrases	Helps me trust God by

Notes, Thoughts, and Questions

_____

_____

_____

_____

Devo 4
Howard

I AM who I AM
READ: Exodus 3:11-15

Scripture Observations

_____

_____

_____

_____

God said to Moses, "I AM WHO I AM.
This is what you are to say to the Israelites:
'I AM has sent me to you.'"
Exodus 3:14

Contemplate the Devotion

Before I AM sends us, I AM calls us. This was Moses' experience. Look back a few verses to verse four. Notice, God drew Moses' attention and when he responded, *God called to him ... "Moses! Moses!"* And Moses did what we should do when the Lord calls. He responded, *"Here I am."* In the story of the conversion of Saul, Ananias responded with identical words when the Lord called him, *"Behold, I am here"* (Acts 9:10 KJV).

Sometimes we don't readily hear that clarion call. Sometimes we are so preoccupied with our desires, our plans, our way of life, that we generate a lot of static. And, like Moses, sometimes when we do hear and we do respond with "Here I am." Then we quickly find reasons, just like Moses did, for why God should not be calling us.

God laid out His plans for Moses. *"I have come down to deliver them from the power of the Egyptians"* (Exodus 3:8a NASB). In my everyday language, this is what I hear God saying. "That's the plan, now come on Moses, get with the program and let's get this job done."

But Moses does what we often do in one way or another. First, he plays the "I am nobody" card saying, "You can't mean me, God, I don't have the gifts, or the training, or the professional status for that." Second, he plays the "I don't have the authority" card.

It is to this latter objection that God says, tell them *"I AM has sent me to you."* But interestingly, being given the authority of God does not satisfy Moses who goes on with a string of objections. Many of us would probably say, "Man, if God came to me in a burning bush I would not question him!"

You and I have been called. We may have experienced some sort of burning bush or we may have heard a soft voice. There may have been a crisis. There may have been a sermon with the threat of hellfire and damnation. But, in some way, there was a call to come to Jesus, along with the call to evangelize and make disciples. And, with that call came the authority of *I AM WHO I AM.*

Our timidity. Our pride. Our lack of training. Our shy and retiring personality. All excuses pale before the calling to come to

Him and to go for Him with the authority of His Name as our mandate and our certificate of authenticity.

Let today be a new beginning. Hear His call and act with His authority.

Prayer

Father, thank You that You have revealed Yourself to us and thank You that You have called me to the task of setting Your people free by declaring Your Gospel. Lord, I surrender all my excuses and beginning today, "Here I am, send me in Your Name!" Amen.

Interact with Biblical Truths (COMPLETE AT LEAST ONE EACH DAY)

➤ List three situations in which you sensed the Lord calling you, yet you used excuses to get out of moving into the situation. What was your excuse?

Situation	Excuses I used

➤ Thinking about the situations you listed, give at least three reasons to overcome your insecurities, fears, or anything else and move into biblically sanctioned situations.

_____

_____

_____

_____

_____

➤ Below are two Old Testament and two New Testament instances of God giving His authority to someone or a group of people. For each instance, to whom did God give His authority, and what is he or they to do with that authority.

God gave His authority to whom	To do what
Deuteronomy 31:7-8	
I Kings 18:22-24	
Matthew 28:18-20	
Luke 9:1	

Notes, Thoughts, and Questions

_____

_____

_____

_____

Getting to know God by His names is

more than simply learning a new word

or discovering a new title He goes by.

His names open up the door

to knowing His character more fully

and experiencing His power more deeply.

~Tony Evans~
"The Power of God's Names"
BeliefNet.com

Devo 5

Shirley

In the beginning was the Word
READ: John 1:1-5

Scripture Observations

_____

_____

_____

_____

In the beginning was the Word,
and the Word was with God, and the Word was God.
John 1:1

Contemplate the Devotion

Today, let's look at the Gospel of John. In our focal passage, we again read the words *In the beginning*. Yet, this time it says, *In the beginning was the Word*. John is talking about Jesus Christ, the second member of the Trinity, present with God the Father and God the Holy Spirit *in the beginning*.

A few verses later John tells us *The Word became flesh and made his dwelling among us. We have seen his glory, the glory of the one and only Son, who came from the Father, full of grace and truth* (John 1:14).

We then read, *and the Word was with God*. Jesus was equal to God, is equal to God … is God. John wants us to be cognizant that the Jesus who turned water into wine and taught on the mountain was God the Son who was with God the Father *in the beginning*, and He is the Savior whose shed blood redeems us.

In the margin of my Bible next to this passage I have written, "In the Word, God revealed Himself and His work. In the Old Testament, God revealed Himself as the One who by His Word spoke creation into being." I do not recall the source of this note, but I do know that God frequently spoke to His prophets and directed them to speak to the people by saying, *Thus says the Lord.* Jewish readers would have understood the phrase *the Word* was important, something to which they should pay attention.

Jesus said, *"You search the Scriptures because you think that in them you have eternal life; and it is they that bear witness about me"* (John 5:39 ESV). In effect, He was saying "You search the words of God to find eternal life, but you do not hear those words speaking about Me." The implication is that they should have understood. John clearly sets forth that Jesus is the very Word of God. He follows this claim with a powerful illustration—Jesus turning water into wine. John then records Jesus' encounter with Nicodemus, illustrating that since Nicodemus was a pharisee in Israel he should know these things. *"You are Israel's teacher,"* said *Jesus, "and do you not understand these things?"* (John 3:10)

Here is what you and I need to hear. *Long ago, at many times and in many ways, God spoke to our fathers ... he has spoken to us by his Son ... through whom also he created the world* (Hebrews 1:1-2 ESV).

Jesus Christ existed before the beginning, walked on the earth as fully God and fully man, was present with God *in the beginning*, is equal to God, and is God. The fact that Jesus Christ is God gives us great strength and comfort as we step into new beginnings.

Prayer

Heavenly Father, thank You for Your Holy Spirit-inspired Word that helps me understand who You are. As I study Your Word, help me know You better, gain a better understanding of what You require of me, and enable me to be obedient to Your Word. May I grow in my faith in You so that I boldly step into the new beginnings and situations ahead. In the Name of Jesus, Amen.

Interact with Biblical Truths (COMPLETE AT LEAST ONE EACH DAY)

➤ List three difficult situations you have faced in the past. What was your reaction to each situation?

Situation	How I reacted
1.	
2.	
3.	

➤ For each situation you listed where your reaction was sinful, How would Christ have you respond in that situation?

How would Christ have me respond.
_____
_____
_____

➤ How does your understanding that Jesus Christ is the very Word of God impact the way you live your life and the choices you make about your new beginnings?

_____

_____

_____

_____

Notes, Thoughts, and Questions

_____

_____

_____

Devo 6

Howard

The light of the world
READ: John 1:9-13

Scripture Observations

_____

_____

_____

_____

"I am the light of the world.
Whoever follows me will not walk in darkness,
but will have the light of life."
John 8:12 (ESV)

Contemplate the Devotion

In the beginning was the Word, and the Word was with God,
and the Word was God.[2] That Word[3] said, *"Let there be light;"*
and there was light.[4] So here in John 8, Jesus claims, *"I am the*
light of the world" and goes on to promise that the one who
follows (believes in or accepts) will not walk in darkness but have
the light of life. Of course, the Pharisees object and attempt to
invalidate His personal witness. You can peruse the commentaries
at another time to consider the technicalities of law embedded in

---

[2] John 1:1 ESV
[3] Colossians 1:16-17
[4] Genesis 1:3

this interchange. Here is the bottom line, so well put by an old standby commentator, Matthew Henry.

> "Christ is the Light of the world. God is light, and Christ is the image of the invisible God. One sun enlightens the whole world; so does one Christ, and there need be no more. What a dark dungeon would the world be without the sun! So would it be without Jesus, by whom light came into the world. Those who follow Christ shall not walk in darkness. They shall not be left without the truths which are necessary to keep them from destroying error, and the directions in the way of duty, necessary to keep them from condemning sin."[5]

When the Lord gave the blueprints for the tabernacle and for formal worship to Israel, the menorah, a golden lampstand, was one of three pieces designated to be in the Holy Place. It was made with one piece of pure hammered gold.

The lampstand had a central branch from which three branches extended on each side, forming a total of seven branches. Seven lamps holding olive oil and wicks stood on top of the branches. Each branch looked like that of an almond tree, containing buds and flowers. The priests were instructed to keep the lamps burning continuously (Leviticus 24:1-30). It is interesting that John is instructed to utilize this imagery in Revelation 2:1 to depict Jesus, … *the One who walks among the*

---

[5] *Matthew Henry's Concise Commentary on the Whole Bible*, John 8:12-16, www.christianity.com/bible/commentary.php?com=mhc&b=43&c=8

seven golden lampstands ... which represent the pastors of the seven churches in Asia Minor.

There is another instructive aspect to the menorah. Did you note that the priests were instructed to keep it filled with oil so that it was never to be without light? That is because the light of the lampstand represented the presence of God, the Light of the World.

Now John exploits this recurring metaphor of light in today's text. In Genesis, the light dispelled the darkness. The flashlight held in your hand to illuminate the key hole so you can unlock your front door dispels the darkness. Such a common activity carries great theological and practical meaning. The theological meaning is this: the Word that was with God spoke light into being, indicating that He is light. This same Word of God proclaims, *"I am the light of the world."*

The practical meaning is this: if we live in darkness, intentionally living out the works of the flesh [6], we can know we are not saved[7]. If we walk in the light, intentionally walking[8] and producing the fruit of the Spirit[9], we are saved. Since we are saved, *the blood of Jesus His Son cleanses us from all sin* (1 John 1:7). Every time we confess our sin Jesus gives us a new beginning (1 John 1:9).

---

[6] Galatians 5:19-21
[7] I John 1:6
[8] Galatians 5:18, 24-25
[9] Galatians 5:22-23

Prayer

Father of the heavenly lights, with whom there is no change or shifting shadow, into Your presence with confidence I come today. Lord, You have set before me life and death and bid me choose life, as Moses challenged the people about to cross into the Promised Land. Throughout Your dealings with Israel You taught them and me that You are light and You dispel darkness. Now Lord, help me to walk in the light as You are in the light by intentionally choosing to walk in the Spirit. Thank You that there is always forgiveness at Your right hand to cleanse me and restore me anew. In Jesus' Name, Amen.

Interact with Biblical Truths (COMPLETE AT LEAST ONE EACH DAY)

➤ As you read today's passage and think about Jesus, the Light of the World, look up the following passages. Explain how each truth gives you hope for living day to day.

This truth gives me hope
Psalm 27:1
John 1:14
John 8:12
John 9:5

➢ List at least three difficult situations that may have occurred in your life. How will remembering that Jesus is the *Light of the World* give you hope in each of the situations?

Difficult situation	It can give me hope by

➢ List at least four ways that Jesus Christ, the Light of the Word, helps you to be a light in the darkness of our world. If you cannot list four ways, reread John 1 for help.

_____

_____

_____

_____

Notes, Thoughts, and Questions

_____

_____

If I am going to use Scripture

to address issues in my life,

I need to know the God behind Scripture.

~Howard Eyrich~

Devo 7

Howard

For all have sinned
READ: Romans 3:21-26

Scripture Observations

_____

_____

_____

_____

For all have sinned and fall short of the glory of God.
Romans 3:23

Contemplate the Devotion

"25 Wrongly-Convicted Felons Exonerated by New Forensic Evidence." What a headline! The story goes on to describe how DNA evidence has changed[10] criminal law and then catalogs twenty-five cases of people wrongly convicted of crimes who were declared not guilty through DNA evidence. Unfortunately though, DNA—our natural man—before the judgment seat of God will not free us; it will condemn us (Romans 3:23).

Have you ever considered the legal structure of the Bible? Before you get through the book of Genesis you are confronted numerous times with this reality. You have the covenant of works with Adam and Eve with complementary judgments for

_____

[10] http://www.forensicsciencetechnician.net/25-wrongly-convicted-felons exonerated-by-new-forensic-evidence/

disobedience. You have the judgment of the flood for the general wickedness of man. You have the gracious covenant with Abraham executed very legally and officially. You have the judgment of Sodom and Gomorrah where Abraham argues the case of the welfare of Lot and his family with the closing statement: *"... will not the judge of all the earth do right?"* (Genesis 18:25)

You have the Ten Commandments and the laws of Moses with their accompanying legal structures. Throughout the Old Testament, the prophets served as prosecuting attorneys representing God in bringing His case against a nation guilty of violating the covenant. In Exodus 32:11-14, Moses becomes the defense attorney on behalf of Israel and wins the case before God.

Your salvation is also pictured in the setting of a courtroom in Romans 4 and 5. With a bit of imagination, you can see God sitting high and lifted up in all His glory, smacking His gavel while proclaiming, "Justified!" because the evidence has been presented that Jesus paid the price of your redemption and His righteousness has been imputed to you (moved to your account).

We live in a litigious society, and most of us would be pleased to never find ourselves before a judge. I once had to appear before a judge in traffic court. A policeman had ticketed me for crossing three lanes of traffic to make a left turn. I decided to contest the ticket and explained to the judge my rationale for the move that generated the ticket. The judge said, "I have done the same thing at that poorly designed intersection. Case dismissed!" He had that power, although his dismissal was not based upon law.

God, however, is both just (operates according to law) and the Justifier (the One who makes the justification possible).

Rejoice today that the Judge of the universe has provided the means whereby He can declare you justified. But also remember that the same God, the Justifier, has provided His rules for living and will once again judge you with respect to your works. This will not be in regard to your salvation and eternal destiny, but it will determine your eternal rewards in heaven (1 Corinthians 3:10-23).

Today is a new day, a new beginning. Petition God for mercy, grace, and empowerment to live by His rules, that you might be ... *adequate, equipped for every good work* (2 Timothy 3:17 NASB), ... *which God prepared beforehand that we should walk in them* (Ephesians 2:10 NASB).

Prayer

Father and judge of all mankind, in the Name of Jesus through the Spirit, I bow my head in humility at the truth that You have declared me just. I am awestruck at the fact that from among billions of people You have called me and given me the faith to trust Jesus so that You might declare me justified. Lord, help me to live a life of gratitude and service starting afresh today. Amen.

Interact with Biblical Truths (COMPLETE AT LEAST ONE EACH DAY)

➢ Explain how understanding sin helps you better understand the gospel.

_____

_____

_____

_____

➢ List at least four ways you will respond to today's Scripture reading.

_____

_____

_____

_____

➢ List at least three ways God has empowered you to be _adequate, equipped for every good work._

_____

_____

_____

_____

Notes, Thoughts, and Questions

_____

_____

_____

But God

READ: Ephesians 2:1-10

Scripture Observations

_____

_____

_____

_____

But God, who is rich in mercy,
because of His great love with which He loved us,
even when we were dead in our trespasses,
made us alive together with Christ (by grace you have been saved).
Ephesians 2:4 & 5b (NKJV)

Contemplate the Devotion

We have already looked at who God is as He has revealed Himself in His Word—the Bible. Everything grows from our knowledge and understanding of who God is, so we must be diligent to read, study, memorize, contemplate, and meditate upon His Word.

Man was made in the image of God and lived a sinless life from the time God created him until he sinned in the Garden of Eden (Genesis 3), and sin has been causing trouble ever since!

Just like Adam and Eve, we often make excuses for our disobedience to God and try to blame other people. And we make excuses for our sin by not recognizing it as sin. When we call sin something other than sin, we begin looking for solutions to the wrong problem. It is only when we recognize sin as sin that we are able to find the only solution to the consequences of sin that we face—forgiveness of those sins through Jesus Christ.

The first three verses of today's passage lay out what we were before we came to saving faith in Christ. We were dead in our trespasses and sins, disobedient children following the desires of our heart, and deserving of God's wrath. Basically, we were lost without any hope!

We often assess a situation to be dire or hopeless. For example, sometimes we wrongly convince ourselves that we are so sinful that God could not possibly save us. Then, we read one of many glorious phrases in Scripture—*But God*—and the whole picture changes!

Today's focal passage reminds us that God is rich in mercy—we don't get what we deserve. Eternal death is what we deserve because of our sin against holy God. We are also reminded not only that God is love, but that He directs His great love toward us. And we are reminded of God's work of kindness: *But* although we deserve punishment and eternal death, *God … made us alive together with Christ* as He redeemed us and made us His children.

The verses that follow remind us that there is nothing we can do to earn our salvation—it is by God's grace we are saved through faith. We then read that we are God's workmanship, new creations created in Jesus Christ for good works.

When teaching this passage, my friend Earle Carpenter

would ask, "Are you wearing your grave clothes? Or are you wearing your grace clothes?" He was asking: "Are you living as if you are still dead in your trespasses and sins, or are you living as a new creation in Christ Jesus?"

Regardless of what we are before coming to Christ, He is willing and able to save us from our hopelessness and deadness, to make us alive in Him by His marvelous work of grace. He makes us a new creation ready to serve Him! And that, my friend is a new beginning indeed!

Prayer

Gracious Heavenly Father, thank You for the reminder that regardless of my past sin, by Your mercy and grace You have given me salvation—new life in You. I pray that I would soak in Your glorious mercy and grace while I live my life as a new creation sharing the gospel with all those who come into my path. In the Name of Jesus I pray, Amen.

INTERACT WITH BIBLICAL TRUTHS: (COMPLETE AT LEAST ONE EACH DAY)

➢ List at least four ways that you can remind yourself that you are a new creation in Christ Jesus.

_____

_____

_____

_____

➤ List ways in which understanding that you are a new creation in Christ Jesus made for good works propels you in your walk as a Christ-follower.

_____

_____

_____

_____

➤ List evidence from your own life that you are still wearing your grave clothes. What are some indications that you are wearing your grace clothes?

Grave clothes evidence	Grace clothes evidence

Notes, Thoughts, and Questions

Marvelous, infinite, matchless grace,

freely bestowed on all who believe;

you that are longing to see his face,

will you this moment His grace receive?

~Julia H. Johnson~
Grace Greater Than Our Sin

Devo 9
Shirley

As far as the east is from the west
READ: Psalm 103:6-14

Scripture Observations

_____

_____

_____

_____

As far as the east is from the west,
so far does He remove our transgressions from us.
Psalm 103:12 (ESV)

Contemplate the Devotion

One morning I noticed an ingrown toenail causing a little irritation on my big toe. I was on my feet a good part of that day, and before long the irritation turned to pain. By that evening my toe was throbbing and felt like I had a needle pushing into my toe. When I finally got home late that night, I pulled off my boots and socks to inspect the toe. It was red, swollen, and, well, I probably shouldn't go into more specific details. The pain radiated upward from my toe, seemingly all the way up to the ends of my hair!

It was time to pull out the pedicure instruments and begin the arduous task of performing an extraction of the ingrown nail before a serious infection set in. Surprisingly, it was not as arduous a task as I had anticipated. In fact, it only took a couple of seconds to slide a cuticle pusher around the edges of the nail to remove the minuscule sliver that had been causing my toe to hurt all day long. I felt immediate relief. Of course, I had to make sure to clean and protect it, and by the next morning the redness, swelling, and most of the pain were gone.

I began thinking of the similarities between that rogue, minuscule sliver of nail and sin in my life. Had I not taken action to remove that sliver of nail, my toe would have become badly infected and the pain would have been unbearable. In a similar way, if I take no action to confess, repent of, and seek forgiveness for my sin, the more pain it will cause and the chasm in my fellowship with God will grow even greater. Eventually the unconfessed sin builds, thus marring my relationship with God and poisoning every aspect of my life. I hurt as a result, and my attitudes and actions often hurt others.

When the cuticle pusher released that sliver of nail I experienced instant relief from the pain it had been causing me throughout the day and evening. When the Holy Spirit convicts us of our sin, we confess and repent, and immediately that sin is removed, *as far as the east is from the west.* We receive God's forgiveness, our relationship with Him is restored, and the weight of that sin is lifted forever.

Just like I had to clear my toe of the sliver and then keep it clean and protected, once we have confessed our sin and received God's forgiveness we must be obedient to God's Word and *be transformed by the renewal of* [our] *minds* (Romans 12:2b) so that healing of our souls is encouraged.

Do you need a sin extraction?

Prayer

Gracious Father, I thank You for Your mercy and grace that is continually poured upon me as You forgive my sins, absolutely and completely. Enable me to be consistent in allowing Your Holy Spirit-inspired Word to convict me of sin and renew my mind as I spend time reading, studying, memorizing, contemplating, and meditating upon Your Word. In the Name of Jesus, Amen.

INTERACT WITH BIBLICAL TRUTHS: (COMPLETE AT LEAST ONE EACH DAY)

➢ Using Scripture, explain what it means that when we are forgiven our sin is removed *as far as the east is from the west.*

_____

_____

_____

_____

➢ What difference does it make in your life that God has compassion on us like a father has compassion on his children (Psalm 103:13)?

_____

_____

_____

_____

➢ In Psalm 103:8-10, David mentions eight character traits of God (NIV). How can remembering each attribute of God help you overcome sin you are facing?

Attribute of God / God is ...	Can help overcome sin by
1. Compassionate	
2. Gracious	
3. Slow to anger	
4. Abounding in love	
5. Not always accusing	
6. Will not be angry forever	
7. Does not treat us how we deserve	
8. Will not repay us or punish us for our sin.	

Notes, Thoughts, and Questions

_____

_____

_____

_____

If sin be removed so far, then we may be sure that the scent,
the trace, the very memory of it must be entirely gone.
If this be the distance of its removal,
there is no shade of fear of its ever being brought back again;
even Satan himself could not achieve such a task.

The Treasury of David
Psalm 103:12
Biblestudytools.com

Devo 10

Shirley

Children of God

READ: 1 John 3:1-10

Scripture Observations

_____

_____

_____

_____

> *See what great love the Father has lavished on us,*
> *that we should be called children of God!*
> *And that is what we are!*
> *The reason the world does not know us*
> *is that it did not know him.*
> 1 John 3:1

Contemplate the Devotion

God is called Father in the Old and New Testaments. Today's Scripture passage reminds us that God the Father's love for us is evident, and it describes the kind of love God has for us.

We are reminded not to take God's love for granted. Because of God the Father's love for us, He gave His only Son Jesus as a sacrifice to save us from our sin and eternal death even though we were His enemies. And He didn't stop there. He showed us His love by bringing us into His family. Imagine that! God calls us His children.

Dear friends of mine adopted a little girl who was four years old. While the legal papers declared this little girl a full part of their family, it took her a while to believe that they wouldn't give her back to the state. It took a while for her to trust her new parents and to feel like she was a part of their family.

God's love is more than signing papers and having a judge declare our adoption finalized; God gives us a new life in Him. In 1 John 3:9 we read, *No one who is born of God will continue to sin, because God's seed remains in them; they cannot go on sinning, because they have been born of God.*

That sounds similar to our reaction to being brought into God's family, doesn't it? God draws us to Himself and declares us His children. At first, we don't really know how to act or what to do. Thankfully, through the Holy Spirit-inspired Word of God and faithful Christ-followers who come alongside us in disciple-making[11] relationships, we begin to know who God is and what we are required to do. And, thankfully, He strengthens and enables us to know Him in such a way that we learn to trust Him.

What exactly does it mean that we are children of God? It means that the Spirit of God lives in us as He leads and transforms us into His image. It means that we do not blend in with the world; instead, we are set apart to show the love of God to the world. It means we are *fellow heirs with Christ*—of all things.

This is amazing, isn't it? Yet, at times we act as though it means absolutely nothing.

As we learn more about what it means to be children of God, we begin to think differently about everything because we develop

---

[11] Making disciple making disciples.

an eternal perspective. An eternal perspective produces grateful hearts as we realize from what and for what we have been saved. As we walk in relationship with Christ, we gain a better understanding of who God is, and what it really means that Christ came to walk this earth as fully God and fully man. Then we know that He brings hope for now and eternity.

Jonathan Edwards is reported to have prayed, "God, stamp eternity on my eyeballs." The idea here is that we have "eternity" branded on our eyes so that we look at all people in view of where they will spend eternity, which leads us to share the gospel with non-Christ-followers in evangelism, and with Christ-followers to encourage them to be His faithful followers. We view every situation we encounter in terms of its eternal significance.

In Scripture we have the assurance of God's love for us, and we learn that love *always protects, always trusts, always hopes, always perseveres* (1 Corinthians 13:7), as well as how to love others. That's a good description of a father's love—particularly of our Heavenly Father's love for His children.

We begin to understand that God is faithful, and we are encouraged to remain faithful and obedient to follow His Word. Father God invites us to bring our concerns to Him. We can come boldly to His throne with all of our concerns, trusting that He will answer them in accordance with His will.

Prayer

Heavenly Father, thank You for loving me so deeply and for the sacrifice You gave to make me Your child. Help me know You better so I will understand more fully what it means to be Your child. Enable me to walk obediently in the love, freedom, and protection You give me. In Jesus' Name, Amen.

Interact with Biblical Truths (COMPLETE AT LEAST ONE EACH DAY)

➤ Give at least three examples from the Bible (with Scripture references) of how God loves His children.

Example	Scripture Reference

➤ Describe at least four ways children of God are to act. How do non-Christ-followers act?

Children of God	Non-Christ-followers

➢ How do you feel when people think you are strange because of your belief in being an adopted child of God? Find biblical promises (give Scripture references) you can stand on to overcome these opinions.

How I feel	Promise I can stand on

Notes, Thoughts, and Questions

_____

_____

_____

_____

I do not stop being a child of God

because I am a problem child.

~Bryan Chapell~
Senior Pastor, Grace Presbyterian Church
Peoria, Illinois

Be holy as I am holy
READ: Leviticus 11:44-47

Scripture Observations

_____

_____

_____

_____

For I am the LORD your God. Consecrate yourselves
therefore, and be holy, for I am holy.
And you shall not make yourselves
unclean with any of the swarming things that swarm on the earth.
Leviticus 11:44 (NKJV)

Contemplate the Devotion

When you read this section of Scripture, if you are like me, you are initially overwhelmed. How can I possibly be holy like God is holy? The answer is in the context: obedience.[12]

What makes God holy? Have you ever thought about this? Most people do not; they simply repeat the words, "God is holy" without the slightest idea of what they are saying other than perhaps that He is sinless. While that is fundamentally correct, another way of thinking about God's holiness is this: all His attributes (sovereignty, mercy, wrath, omnipotence, for example) are in perfect harmony at all times. For example, His mercy is

---

[12] Read Philippians 2:12-18.

never out of sync with His wrath. Thus, God is holy and without sin. Jesus demonstrated this in His life on earth. He lived in perfect obedience—He fulfilled the law in every way and He did the will of the Father at all times; He was obedient.[13]

There is a lot in this passage before us today. We could get lost in attempting to figure out what made certain creatures unclean. We could question why God would make this rule now. "If it was so important, why was it not in place from the beginning? Just what were the swarming things?" These are all good questions and worth studying, but not questions one can answer without significant study. So, if *all Scripture is inspired by God and profitable* (2 Timothy 3:16 NASB), what am I to do with a passage like this?

I am glad you asked, because there is a significant truth in this passage for us without answering all those questions. In fact, the most important truth for us is transparent. This call to Israel to become holy as God is holy is God's call to us as well. The Apostle Peter picks up on this in 1 Peter 1:15 (KJV) when he writes, *But as he which hath called you is holy, so be ye holy in all manner of conversation* [of living].[14]

In the passage before us, God instructs the people through Moses, saying, *"For I am the Lord your God. Consecrate*

---

[13] Read John 14:31 and Hebrews 5:8.

[14] Remember, Peter is writing this to Christian believers dispersed under persecution. He has in view their subjective righteousness. Their objective righteousness has been provided by Christ's perfect righteousness imputed to them at the moment of their justification. Now they are to work out subjective righteousness by choosing obedience so that they accomplish the proof of their faith (James 2:14-16).

yourselves therefore, and be holy, for I am holy." He calls them to a new beginning (one of many times He did that), having them consecrate themselves by changing their diet and behavior.

So, as we come regularly before the Lord to investigate His Word and to commune with Him, He reveals to us areas of our lives that need repentance, or an adjustment in our walk. For example, as a husband or wife you may read Paul's epistle to the Ephesians one morning. You find yourself amazed at all the work God has done to bring you to salvation by grace. Then you come to the fifth chapter and read the instructions to husbands and wives, but now suddenly, they are not just casual instructions, but absolute imperatives. You realize how shallow your love as a husband has been, or how insufficiently you have fulfilled your role as helpmeet to your husband.

God is calling you to consecrate yourself, to be holy as He is holy, by putting aside your self-centeredness (remember the swarming things?) to put on obedience by taking seriously these imperatives in your marriage.

If you are single, you might consider 1 Thessalonians 4:3-9. There you may well be challenged regarding your sexual conduct, understanding that God is calling you to be holy as He is holy with a new beginning of caution.

Consider for a moment today, what are swarming things (the sins that so easily entangle) for you? Hear God's call to a new beginning of holiness in your life with respect to those things. Consecrate yourself to obedience.

Prayer

Father, there is not a single one of us who does not come to Your Word and find a call to consecrate ourselves afresh and thereby, to another new beginning in our walk with You. Help me today to be humble before You and take Your challenge to be holy as you are holy. Amen.

Interact with Biblical Truths (COMPLETE AT LEAST ONE EACH DAY)

➤ Read Psalm 1. What does this psalm teach us to do in order to turn from swarming things? What does this psalm teach us NOT to do.

Psalm 1 says to	Psalm 1 says not to

➢ List each swarming thing in your life. Repent of sin associated with each and consecrate yourself to obedience to God's Word. Write a plan to ward off these swarming things, and how you will be obedient to God's Word?

Swarming things	My plan

➢ Explain how the call to *be holy for I am holy* is a command. How is it also a promise?

How it is a command	How it is a promise

Notes, Thoughts, and Questions

_____

_____

_____

Holiness, as taught in the Scriptures,
is not based upon knowledge on our part.
Rather, it is based upon the resurrected Christ
in-dwelling us and changing us into His likeness.

~A.W. Tozer~

Preparing for Jesus' Return: Daily Live the Blessed Hope

The Son of Man must be lifted up
READ: Numbers 21:4-9

Scripture Observations

_____

_____

_____

_____

"Just as Moses lifted up the snake in the wilderness,
so the Son of Man must be lifted up,
that everyone who believes may have eternal life in him."
John 3:14-15

Contemplate the Devotion

I have always been fascinated by snakes, likely due to spending my childhood in tropical Nigeria, West Africa. Snakes do not scare me, but I do have a healthy respect for them and a proper understanding of how dangerous some snakes are. One of my favorite parts of spending time with fellow Nigeria missionary kids is hearing the now very familiar stories of snake encounters we had in Nigeria.

I think snakes get a bad rap. Yes, the West African green mamba's bite delivers numerous neurotoxins and cardiotoxins that incapacitate the muscles of its prey, paralyzing or killing it. Yet the green mamba is a beautiful green color, a very graceful creature to behold as it navigates through the branches of a tree.

When I hear the biblical accounts of venomous snakes biting and killing the children of Israel, I imagine—even though the geographical habitat is wrong—those snakes were a mix of several West African snakes: black and green mambas, pythons, Gaboon vipers, and black-necked spitting cobras.

Can you imagine how frightening it must have been for the Israelites when all those poisonous snakes slithered into their camp and started biting them? To us, that sounds like pretty harsh discipline from God, doesn't it? Well, not really, when we realize the depth of their sin against God.

Once the people realized their sin, they came to Moses and asked Him to pray that the Lord would take the snakes away from their camp and save them from those venomous bites. Moses once again interceded for God's people, and God provided a way for them to be saved from the snakes. Moses instructed the people to make a bronze snake and place it on a pole in the midst of the camp. Then he told them that when they were bitten they should look up at the bronze snake and they would live.

The context for today's focal passage is the interaction between Jesus and Nicodemus (John 3:1-15). In explaining what the "Kingdom of God" is, Jesus tells Nicodemus that *no one can see the kingdom of God unless they are born again.* As Jesus continued he made an analogy using an Old Testament passage that Nicodemus, who had studied Scripture and history, would understand. Jesus knew the Old Testament too, and understood that everything in it pointed to Him. But, for Jesus to actually compare Himself—the Son of Man—to a snake was, and is, a bit jarring.

The verse that follows in this account, John 3:16, is one of the best known in the world: *For God so loved the world that he gave his one and only son, that whosoever believes in him shall not perish but have eternal life.*

The bronze snake in Numbers 21 is compared to Christ on the cross and the greatness of His love and mercy. "Jesus became what we are that we might become what He is."[15]

Did you observe these truths in the Old and New Testament accounts? In the Old Testament narrative God sent His wrath, in the form of venomous snakes, because of the sinful rebellion of His people. In the New Testament we learn that God's wrath is poured out on non-Christ-followers in their eternal death.

In Numbers 21 the people were already bitten and the venom was in their bodies working to kill them. They would die without God's intervention. God did not remove the snakes nor the Israelites from the camp—He provided a way for them to be saved from the venomous bites of the snakes. Before coming to Christ, sin had poisoned us and there was nothing we could do to save ourselves.

The very thing that was killing the Israelites—snakes—is what God used to save them. In the same way that the people could only be saved by looking at the bronze snake, we can only be saved by looking up to the Son of Man, Jesus, bearing all of our sin

---

[15] Athanasius of Alexandria

as He is crucified and dies on the cross. The Israelites had to do one thing to be saved from the outpouring of God's wrath: look up at the bronze snake hanging on the pole. In a similar way, we must look up to the cross of Jesus for our salvation. Yet, we cannot leave Jesus dead on the cross, because He defeated death when He arose victoriously, and then He ascended into heaven where He sits at the right hand of the throne of God interceding for us (Romans 8:34).

As Christ-followers we are to look to Jesus at all times for guidance, strength, and provision. And, while most of us don't face being surrounded by venomous snakes, we often find ourselves in dire situations where the rug gets pulled out from under us and we cannot wrap our minds around what is happening or what has happened to us. We often tend to focus—and sometimes obsess— on all of these things, and the more we focus on them the more frantic we become. During these dire times and as we face new beginnings, we are to *throw off everything that hinders and the sin that so easily entangles*, by *fixing our eyes on Jesus*, our only hope (Hebrews 12:1-2).

Prayer

Father, thank You for Your saving mercy, grace, love, and patience, and for the reminders throughout Your Word that point me to salvation through Your Son, Jesus. Enable me to focus my heart, mind, and eyes on You in the midst of everything I face. In the Name of Jesus, Amen.

Interact with Biblical Truths (COMPLETE AT LEAST ONE EACH DAY)

➢ List at least two situations in your life when God provided a way for you to be saved instead of removing you from the situation, or removing the situation. Explain your reaction to each situation.

Situation	My reaction

➢ For the situations listed above, what did you learn about God and yourself as a result of your not being removed from the situation or the situation not being removed?

_____

_____

_____

➢ Explain how the account of the bronze serpent helps you better understand why Jesus came to earth to live as fully God and fully man.

_____

_____

_____

Notes, Thoughts, and Questions

_____

_____

_____

_____

God has been speaking to mankind since the
Garden of Eden (Hebrews 1:1-2).
Throughout the history of the Old Testament
He spoke more and more through the prophets,
but in Jesus, He came in flesh and spoke
by His life and by His words.
Little wonder Jesus finished His encounter
with Nicodemus with these words:
And as Moses lifted up the serpent in the wilderness,
so must the Son of Man be lifted up,
that whoever believes in him may have eternal life.
(John 3:14-15)

~Howard Eyrich~

Devo 13
Howard

Walk by the Spirit

Scripture Observations

_____

_____

_____

_____

But I say, walk by the Spirit,
and you will not gratify the desires of the flesh.
Galatians 5:16 (ESV)

Contemplate the Devotion

In these verses, we learn about the fruit of the Spirit. Notice that the word fruit is singular. When we lived in Miami we would sometimes send a crate of citrus fruit to friends for a holiday gift. The crate would read something like "Florida Citrus Fruit," and inside would be grapefruit, oranges, and other assorted varieties of citrus fruit. So, the Holy Spirit gives us His crate marked LOVE which includes a variety of expressions of love—joy, peace, patience, kindness, goodness, faithfulness, gentleness, self-control—all fruit of the Spirit.

However, as one studies the Bible an interesting anomaly appears. We are called upon to develop this same fruit as character traits in our lives. For example, consider these illustrations:

- John 13:34—Jesus tells us that He gives us a new command: *Love one another.*

- Romans 12:18—Paul exhorts us to *be at peace with one another.*

- Philippians 4:4—Paul challenges us to *rejoice always, and again I say rejoice.*

- Colossians 3:12—Paul challenges us to *put on kindness, longsuffering, and patience.*

Surprisingly, what we learn is that these character traits are a gift of the Holy Spirit, but we are responsible to choose to live them out in daily life. When my friends received the crate that we sent to them, they needed to open it and partake of the fruit. As believers, we need to partake of the fruit of the Spirit.

Consider Colossians 3:12 (KJV), which begins with a command; *Put on therefore.* This was a common Greek phrase that a mother would use to instruct a child on a wintry morning, "It is cold, put on therefore your coat!"

If your son is going to properly dress for the day, he must choose the appropriate clothing from the selection in the closet. Once that selection is made, he still needs to reach into the closet, take those clothes off the hanger, and slip them onto his body! The clothing will not jump out of the closet and onto his body without his engagement. If he is going to wear them, he must put them on.

Here is the point that Paul is making. If you're going to show love, joy, peace, patience, kindness, goodness, faithfulness, gentleness, and self-control toward other people, you must make a choice to act in this fashion! Such Christian walking is just as much a choice as it is to choose and walk in weather-appropriate clothing. If you don't choose to put on this fruit of the Spirit and walk in it, you won't do it!

When so challenged, people often object by saying something like, "I tried that and I can't do it!" Or, "If it is the fruit of the Spirit and the Holy Spirit lives in me then it should be natural, so I must not be a Christian." However, some in-depth discussion with the individual will usually reveal that the Holy Spirit has been grieved by his choice to not put on the clothing (fruit) He has provided (Ephesians 4:29-32).

Today, my friend, open this crate of fruit that the Apostle Paul has sent to you and experience a new beginning in your Christian walk. Choose (you have the promise that the indwelling Holy Spirit will enable you) to put on love, joy, peace, patience, kindness, goodness, faithfulness, gentleness, self-control; and choose to put off all those things Paul lists in Ephesians 4:31; namely, bitterness, wrath, anger, clamor, slander, and malice. To do so calls for confession of your sin and repentance—the decision to turn from works of the flesh (Galatians 5:19-21).

Prayer

Father, so often we struggle with the simple fundamentals of living the Christian life. I am so accustomed to instant gratification that I desire my Christian life to be microwave-quick. I have heard so often that I cannot do anything without You, so I end up doing nothing. Yet Your Word is clearly full of imperatives, along with the promises of Your enabling. Lord, help me to choose to open the crate of fruit that the Holy Spirit is delivering and choose to be obedient to love and be patient and kind, expecting that Your Spirit will enable me to obediently do so. And, Father, convict me where my desire is weak. Draw me near through Your Word and fill me with Your Spirit so that my heart desires to follow You and You alone. Amen.

Interact with Biblical Truths (COMPLETE AT LEAST ONE EACH DAY)

➤ For each of the character traits given, either write how it manifests itself in your life, or, write what bad character trait is manifested in your life instead.

In what situation would living out this character trait be helpful
John 13:34—*love one another*
Romans 12:18—*be at peace with one another*
Philippians 4:4—*rejoice always, and again I say rejoice*
Colossians 3:12— *put on kindness, longsuffering, and patience*

➤ For each fruit of the Spirit, either write how it manifests itself in your life, or, write what bad fruit is manifested in your life instead.

Fruit of the Spirit	How it manifests itself / Bad fruit that manifests instead
Love	
Joy	
Peace	
Kindness	
Goodness	
Faithfulness	
Gentleness	
Self-Control	

➢ Pray, asking forgiveness for the bad fruit in your life. For each of the fruit of the Spirit, write a biblical plan to nurture any of the underdeveloped fruit in your life. Give Scripture references.

My plan to nurture these underdeveloped fruit
Love
Joy
Peace
Kindness
Goodness
Faithfulness
Gentleness
Self-Control

Notes, Thoughts, and Questions

_____

_____

_____

_____

Instead of saying

"Here's the standard … now live UP TO IT"

the Apostle Paul encourages the believer

to "live OUT OF" the Gospel

through the power of the indwelling Holy Spirit.

~Paul David Tripp~
"Walk in a Manner Worthy"
Paultripp.com

When you pass through the waters
READ: Isaiah 43:1-7

Scripture Observations

_____

_____

_____

_____

When you pass through the waters, I will be with you;
And when you pass through the rivers,
they will not sweep over you.
When you walk through the fire, you will not be burned;
the flames will not set you ablaze.
Isaiah 43:2

Contemplate the Devotion

In a two-week period, two families of close acquaintance shared a common tragedy. Both families lost young adult children; one to a freak accident of nature and the other to the nasty disease of cancer. Another ministry worker and I had a lengthy conversation with one of the dads. He shared the incredible journey of faith that they walked through for two years of illness and the literally hundreds of opportunities for ministry to others that came through the course of the cancer.

Some years ago, I walked this pathway with a good friend of thirty plus years. A nasty strain of cancer, generated through contact with a defoliating agent, ate away his insides. He was the father of three young adult children. Not long before he died, I visited him in a specialty hospital far from his home. His wife and I stood by his bed when he asked for help to get to the bathroom. As we assisted him his gown slipped off his body leaving him fully exposed. It was an emotionally difficult experience for all three of us as his dignity dissolved in our embarrassment. Several weeks later we buried him.

How does one process such experiences? Our text today goes to the very heart of the answer. As believers, we have confidence in the promises of God as we see them exemplified in this text. Yes, the context is the Word of the Lord to Israel. However, elsewhere in Scripture, God tells us many times that He is our creator and that He formed us in the womb. The promises made here to Israel—the waters *will not overflow you* and *you will not be scorched* (by the fire of trials)—are metaphors that parallel those of the New Testament.

If you are familiar with the history of Israel, you know that these promises have been individually fulfilled in part on several occasions, but the total fulfillment is yet ahead of Israel. Likewise, with us, these promises are fulfilled to us individually from time to time in lesser or greater degrees. In the loss of a child, the waters do overflow us, but not totally. As we walk by faith and trust His Sovereign Divine Providence, the waters settle and they do not overwhelm us.

Yes, again, this passage is about Israel, but a careful extended reading of the chapter leaves no doubt that while there is specificity to Israel, all believers are in view. My friend's three children have grown up to walk with the Lord. Their father would be grateful to God for the way they walk the Christian life. His widow continued to serve the Lord until her retirement from the ministry agency with which they were associated. Life has certainly been different than they anticipated, but the waters have not overflowed them nor the fire consumed them.

I have full confidence that my recently suffering friends will not be overwhelmed, because they have been living life by abiding in Christ. His grace will be their portion. Another man with whom I walked as he cared for his wife and then lost her to cancer illustrates how the Lord brings new beginnings out of such painful events. This fellow buried his wife and grieved her death appropriately. Three or four years later he remarried, and they have made a lovely home for his children. No, these new beginnings are not without struggles, but they are nonetheless new beginnings. They are horizontal redemptions and rebirths. They remind us that we are precious in His sight.

Therefore, determine today that "whate'er befall" you, you will live by this injunction: *"Do not fear, for I have redeemed you,"* promises *"the Holy One of Israel, your Savior"* (Isaiah 43:1, 3). Remember the miracles at the hands of Moses and Joshua, or Elijah and Elisha, and then remember this declaration, *Jesus Christ is the same yesterday and today and forever* (Hebrews 13:8 ESV).

Prayer

Father, You are sovereign over the tragedies of life. You can and will enable me to walk by faith and display Your grace. I am grateful to be Your witness when my life is put under the pressures of living in a fallen world. Grant, Lord, that others will be encouraged that they too can have new beginnings even as they observe You bringing new beginnings out of the agonies in my life. Amen.

Interact with Biblical Truths (COMPLETE AT LEAST ONE EACH DAY)

> List at least three difficult situations that have occurred in your life. How can remembering that God has redeemed you and will be with you always have given you hope in each of these situations?

Difficult situation	It gives me hope by

➢ Read the passages below. Explain how the truth in each passage gives you hope for living day to day.

This truth gives me hope
Isaiah 41:10
Luke 21:28
1 Corinthians 1:30
Hebrews 13:8
1 Peter 1:18-19

➤ How does your understanding that you have been redeemed by God impact the way you live your life and the choices you make?

_____

_____

_____

_____

Notes, Thoughts, and Questions

_____

_____

_____

_____

Devo 15
Shirley

Consider it pure joy
READ: James 1:2-8

Scripture Observations

_____

_____

_____

_____

> *Consider it pure joy, my brothers and sisters,*
> *whenever you face trials of many kinds,*
> *because you know that the testing of your*
> *faith produces perseverance.*
> James 1:2-3

Contemplate the Devotion

In today's reading, James, the half-brother of Jesus, reminds his readers of something they have been taught before—Christ-followers grow through difficulties. Yet, James knew they needed to hear it again. Why? Because he understood that there is a big difference in knowing something and actually putting that knowledge into practice.

We have to be taught that God uses difficulties to strengthen our faith and develop endurance. Without knowing this important truth, our reaction to the *trials of many kinds* is likely to fall very short of joy.

During our lifetime, we face many difficult situations. When those situations hit us, we have a choice to make. Do we respond in a godly manner by choosing joy? Or do we react in an ungodly manner by getting angry or disappointed with God, and perhaps even other people?

My quintessential example of a person exhibiting "the joy of the Lord" is my mom. Regardless of the circumstances in which she landed—many very difficult, painful, and dangerous situations— she chose joy. The joy of the Lord radiated brilliantly upon her face. Those who knew my mom can picture in their mind's eye her beautiful, sparkling, and joyful countenance that brightened up the room. Do not misunderstand me, she was not joyful that the difficulty was upon her, she was joyful because she knew God was in control and that the difficulty would help root out unconfessed sin in her life, strengthen her faith, and produce endurance for the difficulties to come.

Here it is important to tell you that mom, like everyone else, shed many tears and grieved over many things. Yet, in the midst of the tears and grieving, the joy of the Lord was ever present.

That Thursday morning, as word spread that Mom would soon be going home to heaven, the hospital room and hallways began to fill with countless family and friends. Our phones were ringing as people called, and we received dings alerting us to texts and emails from all over the world.

At one point, I walked from the hallway where I had been talking with some friends, and stepped into her room. There she sat propped up in the bed, receiving family and friends as if she were a queen. As friends left they would comment, "I can't believe she is so close to death. You would never know she is in so much pain."

How was it possible for this eighty-six-year-old woman, who was in excruciating pain and having difficulty breathing, to be joyful? Throughout her life Mom believed, and taught all of us—and the watching world on two continents—to live out Colossians 2:6-7: *So then, just as you received Christ Jesus as Lord, continue to live your lives in him, rooted and built up in him, strengthened in the faith as you were taught, and overflowing with thankfulness.*

Mom had a close relationship with her Savior and Lord, Jesus. Because of her deep, abiding faith in Him, she was *rooted and built up in him* which resulted in her being *strengthened in* [her] *faith* so that she was a pillar of strength in the midst of any difficulty or turmoil. As a result, she responded to those difficulties with joy and a grateful heart. Regardless of how little she had or how difficult the situation in which she found herself, she was always thankful for the Lord's love, grace, mercy, provision, and strength.

Prayer

Heavenly Father, I thank You for Your love, mercy, and grace that allows me to walk through the difficulties in my life so that my faith is strengthened. Enable me to be consistent in being obedient to Your Word that You use to grow deep roots of faith in my life. In the Name of Jesus, Amen.

Interact with Biblical Truths (COMPLETE AT LEAST ONE EACH DAY)

➤ Think of a Christ-following friend who is going through a very difficult time. Write a plan for how you can encourage him or her to stand firm in his or her faith in the midst of the difficulty.

_____

_____

_____

➤ Think of a very difficult time (spiritual, emotional, mental, or physical) in your life. Briefly explain that difficulty, and how you reacted/responded to it.

Difficulty	How I reacted/responded

➤ For the situation you explained, if you reacted in an ungodly manner, write a plan of how you could have made that ungodly reaction into a godly response, giving Scripture passages that relate to each point of your plan.

My plan	Scripture passages

Notes, Thoughts, and Questions

_____

_____

_____

_____

If you are living in the grip of bitterness
because of things that happened to you in the past,
there is hope and freedom in the grace, mercy, love,
and forgiveness of our Savior, Jesus Christ.

~Shirley Crowder~

Devo 16

Shirley

But God meant it for good

READ: Genesis 50:19-21

Scripture Observations

_____

_____

_____

_____

> *As for you, you meant evil against me,*
> *but God meant it for good, to bring it about*
> *that many people should be kept alive,*
> *as they are today.*
> Genesis 50:20 (ESV)

Contemplate the Devotion

The biblical account of Joseph has always fascinated me. I am the youngest of four siblings, and, although our experience didn't involve a lot of sibling rivalry, I understand very well how arguments and jealousies arise.

Today's reading is a small portion of the entire account of Joseph's life. His life as his father's favored son was ideal. Everything seemed to be going in Joseph's favor until he was sold into slavery by his brothers. This set into motion a series of very difficult events in Joseph's life. Interspersed among these horrible events we read: *The LORD was with Joseph* (Genesis 39:2 ESV).

After Joseph had been in jail for two years, Pharaoh had a dream, but none of his wise men could interpret the dream for him. Then, the cupbearer who had been in jail with Joseph, told the Pharaoh that Joseph could interpret his dream. Pharaoh summoned Joseph who did interpret the dream and Pharaoh made him second in command to prepare Egypt for the coming famine.

Fast forward seven years to when the drought hit the land and Joseph's brothers came to Egypt for food. The chapters that follow tell of Joseph providing for his family and being reunited with his father, Jacob. The children of Israel then moved to Egypt and prospered under the care of Joseph.

As we pick up the account in today's reading, we find that Jacob has died. Joseph's brothers are afraid now that their father is dead, Joseph will decide to take revenge on them for selling him into slavery. They come to Joseph to beg for mercy. The fact that they thought Joseph would do them harm brings tears to Joseph's eyes.

Joseph tells them that it's God's job to judge them, not his. And then he tells them that what they intended for evil (selling him into slavery), God used for good (to provide for them, their families, and all of Egypt).

Joseph treated them lovingly and mercifully. There was no anger, bitterness, or hatred toward his brothers. He responded in forgiveness and compassion.

How in the world was Joseph able to respond to his brothers in kindness, love, mercy, and grace? We see several biblical truths involved here.

First of all, Joseph knew God was God. Even though his position as second in command directly under Pharaoh gave him great power in Egypt, he didn't try to take God's place as judge. When he said, *"Am I in God's place?"* (Genesis 50:19 ESV), Joseph was saying, "It's God's job to judge you, brothers, not mine."

Joseph tells his brothers, "You meant it for evil when you sold me into slavery; *but God meant it for good*." Joseph is talking about God's providence, meaning that God works in and through every situation to bring about His will—regardless of the good or bad intentions of people.

Joseph also understood that God was at work in and through everything that was happening to him—he understood the sovereignty and providence of God. His understanding of who God is produced a grateful heart within him.

When we walk with God, we understand that God is in control and working everything for His glory and our good (Romans 8:28). That knowledge enables us to walk through the suffering, pain, and trials, empowered by God's strength.

Even though we may not understand what is happening in our lives, we can always know that God is in control.

Prayer

Heavenly Father, thank You for allowing me to look at the life of Joseph, since it is such a clear picture of Your control over everything. Help me know You better so that in the midst of my struggles I will trust You. In the Name of Jesus I pray, Amen.

Interact with Biblical Truths (COMPLETE AT LEAST ONE EACH DAY)

➢ Although we are not specifically told what Joseph did to develop mercy, grace, love, and kindness in his heart, his actions show us that they were present. Give examples from today's reading and from other Scripture passages that describe the life of Joseph, exhibiting each characteristic.

Examples
Mercy
Grace
Love
Kindness

➢ Often, our sinfully angry reactions to people and situations grow deep roots of bitterness in our hearts. In Romans 12:14-21 you will find things that you are to do and not do in order to stop bitterness from growing in your heart. List them.

Do these things	Don't do these things

➢ Now list some things that "kill" these characteristics in your heart.

Characteristic killers
Mercy
Grace
Love
Kindness

Notes, Thoughts, and Questions

_____

_____

_____

_____

The fact that God can bring good out of evil
only underscores the power and excellence
of His Sovereign will.

~R. C. Sproul~
Ligonier Ministries

Forgiving one another
READ: Ephesians 4:25-32

Scripture Observations

_____

_____

_____

_____

*And be kind and compassionate to one another,
forgiving one another, just as in Christ God forgave you.*
Ephesians 4:32

Contemplate the Devotion

Today we are looking at forgiveness. In the context of church discipline in Matthew 18, Peter asks the question, "How many times should I forgive my brother, up to seven times?" Jesus' answer no doubt startled him. To put it in today's casual language, Jesus asked, "Peter, how about you forgive him seventy times seven?" Why did Peter say seven times? Amos tells of God forgiving Israel three times before He punished them. Jewish leaders doubled that amount, and Peter added one more time for good measure.

When Jesus proposes 490 times he is, in effect, saying there is no limit on the expectation to forgive. To make sure that Peter, the rest of the disciples, and we, do not miss the point, Jesus continues with a parable. In this story, a servant owes the king 10,000 talents (probably about $300,000 in today's US currency) and the servant does not have the money to repay him. The king forgives his debt. The servant then goes out and throws a fellow servant into prison because he cannot repay a hundred denarii (about ten cents). Jesus purposefully exaggerates the numbers to make His point.

In the Biblical Counseling Center where I worked for the final twenty years of my career, we saw many people who struggled with forgiveness. These folks included wives who discovered husbands with severe pornography addictions, husbands with wives committing adultery, teenagers suffering from the divorce of parents, as well as people dealing with a variety of other offenses. What can a counselor, or any Christ-follower, do to help these people?

Paul lays out the remedy that is elsewhere developed in Scripture as well, that the offended is to forgive as God (the offended one) has forgiven him or her (the offender). God made a choice to set in motion the exquisite plan of salvation in which he provided the basis of redemption. We must make a choice. God put your sin (offense) *as far away as the east is from the west* (Psalm 103:12) or buried it in the deepest sea (Micah 7:19). Consequently, we need to choose to put the offense out of our minds and remember it no more.

Anyone who is married and is honest knows the truth of this matter. Two sinners living in the intimacy of marriage must practice forgiveness as a way of life. Two roommates, two neighbors, two soldiers on a mission, must learn to do likewise. Walking together while not practicing forgiveness will generate bitterness. So, beloved, remember that love (forgiveness) covers a multitude of sin (1 Peter 4:8).

Mary Katherine discovered that her husband visited prostitutes on several occasions. This is an offense that seems gargantuan to forgive and put out of one's mind. However, George repented and demonstrated the fruit of repentance over an extended period (Matthew 3:8). They both grew in their walk with the Lord. George sought forgiveness and Mary Katherine forgave him. Their marriage was renewed—a new beginning for them. Forgiveness always engenders a new beginning.

Prayer

Father, thank You that You set the standard of forgiveness in sending Your Son to die in my place and giving me His righteousness. Now, Father, help me to listen to You and follow Your example—sometimes it is a small offense that simply generates hurt feelings and other times it is seemingly an impossible situation like Mary Katherine faced. Lord, whatever the challenge, help me to practice forgiving and to develop a forgiving spirit. Amen.

Interact with Biblical Truths (COMPLETE AT LEAST ONE EACH DAY)

➤ Describe what it means to forgive someone.

_____

_____

_____

_____

➤ Write at least three situations when you had (or are having) a struggle forgiving someone for an offense. Tell what made (makes) it so difficult to forgive the offense.

Difficult situations to forgive	Why was it so difficult to forgive?
1.	
2.	
3.	

➢ Beside the number corresponding to each difficult situation, write "Yes" if this issue is resolved; write "No" if the issue is not resolved. If the issue is resolved, write how you resolved the issue; if it remains unresolved, write a plan to resolve the issue.

Resolved? Yes / No	How it was resolved / Plan to resolve
1.	
2.	
3.	

Notes, Thoughts, and Questions

_____

_____

_____

_____

Forgiveness withheld
    A poison potion.
Forgiveness extended
    A sweet honeycomb.
Forgiveness received
    Salve for the soul.
Forgiveness rejected
    A fool's choice.

~Howard Eyrich~

Devo 18
Shirley

But if not
READ: Daniel 3:8-18

Scripture Observations

_____

_____

_____

_____

> *"But if not, be it known to you, O king,*
> *that we will not serve your gods*
> *or worship the golden image that you have set up."*
> Daniel 3:18 (ESV)

Contemplate the Devotion

I have a sketchy memory of being taught the account of Shadrach, Meshach, and Abednego by one of my Nigeria missionary uncles. He read the account from his Bible, and then he and several other missionary uncles reenacted it for the missionary kids (MKs).

The king was dressed as a Nigerian Oba (king) in a traditional brightly colored agbada (long, flowing robe that fits over their clothes) and he wore a gold paper crown. The image of Nebuchadnezzar was an ebony statue also wearing a gold paper crown.

I can still see and hear several parts of the reenactment. When the servants brought Shadrach, Meshach, and Abednego before the king, he asked, in Nigerian Pidgin, "You no dey hear word?" (i.e., "Didn't you get the message that you are to bow down to my statue?")

When the three men were about to be thrown into the furnace they said to the king, "Please sah, God He fit save us. But if He no go do am, we no go serve your own gods and we no go worship idols."

And then, when the king noticed there were four men in the furnace, he slapped each side of his head with his hands while saying, "Ah! Ah!" (i.e., for goodness' sake). When the three men came out of the furnace, the king walked over to them and touched their hair, touched and sniffed their clothes. When he discovered their hair was not singed, and they did not smell of smoke the king said, "It is wandaful!"

While we MKs were very entertained by this reenactment, this precious memory planted seeds of trusting God in my heart, regardless of the circumstances.

It is unlikely that any of us will face being thrown into a literal fiery furnace; however, we will face fiery trials (1 Peter 4:12-13). How do we prepare ourselves to stand firm in the midst of the fiery trials we face? We must be diligent to read, study, memorize, contemplate, and meditate upon the Word of God so that we come to know Him and His character as we walk in obedience to His commands. In turn, our faith in God is strengthened to enable us to trust Him to carry us through these fiery trials.

And, because our faith in God is so strong, we are able to say, along with Shadrach, Meshach, and Abednego, "God is able and will deliver us." And furthermore, to say with just as much certainty, "But if God chooses not to deliver us, we will not dishonor and disobey Him by worshiping your idols."

These fiery trials help sanctify us. Talking about fiery trials always reminds me of the third verse of the hymn, *How Firm a Foundation*.[16]

> When thro' fiery trials thy pathway shall lie,
>
> My grace, all-sufficient, shall be thy supply;
>
> The flame shall not hurt thee; I only design
>
> Thy dross to consume, and thy gold to refine.

Do you know how gold is refined? It is refined by fire that melts the gold and brings all the impurities (what is not gold) to the top. The impurities are skimmed off and discarded, and the process continues until the impurities are gone.

Similarly, a great deal of refining occurs in the life of a Christ-follower. As the Lord works in and through the circumstances of our lives, often "turning up the heat," our sin comes to the surface. As the Holy Spirit convicts us of our sin and leads us to repentance, our sin is removed. This process we call sanctification continues throughout our lives.

We need to pray that God would refine us like gold is refined by turning up the heat so that the impurities (sin) in our hearts

---

[16] Many attribute this hymn to George Keith. In John Rippon's *A Selection of Hymns* (1787), *How Firm a Foundation* (no. 128) is attributed simply to "K—".

would be recognized as sin against holy God. Then we need to be quick to confess, repent of that sin, and walk in the freedom of God's forgiveness.

Prayer

Father, please show me areas of my life in which I am not standing firm against the pressures of the world. Strengthen my faith to stand firm in the midst of every situation so the watching world will glorify you as King Nebuchadnezzar did. In Jesus' Name, Amen.

Interact with Biblical Truths (COMPLETE AT LEAST ONE EACH DAY)

➤ List at least four things the world pressures you to worship. Then explain how you have stood firm and not given in to that pressure. If you have not stood firm to withstand these pressures, write a plan to help you not give in to that pressure in the future.

The world pressures me to worship	I have stood firm / My plan to stand firm

➤ How did Shadrach, Meshach, and Abednego prepare themselves to stand firm in their faith in God? (See Daniel 2.)

_____

_____

_____

_____

➤ Describe a demonstration of faith in God you have observed or heard about. Explain how that demonstration of faith affected you, your Christ-following friends, and the watching world.

_____

_____

_____

_____

Notes, Thoughts, and Questions

_____

_____

_____

_____

If I am stepping into a lion's den
I want to know who the lions are.

(Pastor taking a new call to a somewhat troubled church.)

Lions are lions and God is God.
If he puts you in the lion's den he can shut their mouths.

(His mentor's response.)

Devo 19
Shirley

Therefore I have hope
READ: Lamentations 3:21-24

Scripture Observations

_____

_____

_____

_____

This I recall to mind, therefore I have hope.
Lamentations 3:21 (ESV)

Contemplate the Devotion

In the Bible, we find passages telling us to recall or remember who God is. What does it mean to *recall to mind*? It means that you have had something in your mind in the past, and now you bring it back into your present thought processes. A key here is that in order to be reminded of something, you have to already have that information in your mind.

In the Old Testament, people built altars to signify and remind them of God's work in their lives or the lives of His people. In addition to the Bible, my prayer journal serves as a reminder of God's work in my life and the lives of my family and friends. Before stepping into a major new beginning—new year, new job, new project—it is my practice to read through my prayer journals. These readings remind me of God's faithfulness, mercy, grace, and love that has enabled me to walk through every situation I encountered.

Today's reading follows the descriptions of the affliction and misery occurring in Jerusalem because of God's judgment on His disobedient people. We read, *This I recall to mind* …. "This" refers to what we read in the next verses, God's faithfulness and His mercies.

Isn't that interesting? Instead of focusing on all the misery, the focus is on God's faithfulness and His mercies. Hope comes from remembering who God is and His character.

I often hear people say, "I hope against hope …." According to the site for Merriam Webster, "hope against hope" means "to hope without any basis for expecting fulfillment." Basically, it means hope is useless. If there is nothing on which to base the expectation that hope will be fulfilled, is that really hope?

As we walk in relationship with Christ, we gain a better understanding of who God is, and what it really means that Christ came to walk this earth as fully God and fully man. That is the basis of our expectation that our hope in God will be fulfilled—here on earth and for eternity.

Recall the truth that there is NO hope outside of a personal relationship with Jesus Christ; and, that the hope Christ brings is everlasting! Edward Mote wrote the words for the hymn, *The Solid Rock*. It is based on 1 Corinthians 3:11, *Because no one can lay any other foundation, than what has been laid—that is, Jesus*

Christ. The chorus tells us "On Christ, the solid Rock, I stand; All other ground is sinking sand."

Praise God that our hope is firmly placed in Him for our present, future, and for eternity.

Prayer

Thank You, Father, that my hope is in You. Help me remember Your faithfulness and mercies as I move forward into my new beginnings. May I walk into the future with the confidence that You are my Savior—my hope! In Jesus' Name, Amen.

Interact with Biblical Truths (COMPLETE AT LEAST ONE EACH DAY)

➤ Think of a new beginning in your life. Describe how reminding yourself of God's faithfulness, mercy, grace, and love enabled you to walk into and through that new beginning with confidence and hope.

_____

_____

_____

_____

➤ List some hurts or disappointments in your past. Find and list reminders from God's Word of His promises and character that can help you overcome each hurt and disappointment.

Hurts / Disappointments	God's promises and character

> Briefly describe some situations about which you are harboring disappointment, anger, hatred, or bitterness. Confess your sin to the Lord and seek His forgiveness. Make a plan for seeking forgiveness from those whom you may have sinned against in each situation, if feasible.

Situation	My plan

Notes, Thoughts, and Questions

Hope returns when the sufferer turns his heart
back to the truth of the Word of God
and the faithful character of God.

~Paul Tautges~
The Discipline of Mercy

Be on the alert
READ: Colossians 1:21-23

Scripture Observations

_____

_____

_____

_____

Be on the alert, stand firm in the faith,
act like men, be strong.
1 Corinthians 16:13 (NASB)

Contemplate the Devotion

A young man of close acquaintance grew up as an only child on an isolated farm. He was a bright fellow, but in today's world he would have been diagnosed with moderate learning disabilities. As a result, his reading skills developed slowly and school was a chore. His best friend was his dog. They spent many a happy hour roaming the hundreds of acres of farmland and woods available.

As he reached his teen years, he was introduced to the vices that plague so many. He says he is thankful that recreational drugs were not part of his culture. Drinking became his pathway to escaping the pain of his social ineptness. It also determined his social context. His godly mother lived in deep sorrow and confident faith. She learned from the Apostle Paul to never cease praying for her son.

One day the drinking led to a serious auto accident resulting in a shattered elbow and a hospital stay. On the morning after the accident, there appeared a front-page article in the newspaper about another teenager involved in a similar accident, whose arm was torn from his body. That report certainly grabbed my friend's attention—his mother's God had been kind to him.

Having no car brought renewed isolation into his life. His friends evaporated. One of those friends said, "You don't expect me to drive my freshly washed wheels in and out of that mile of dirt road to pick you up and go pick up our dates, do you?"

As he considered these things, he concluded it was time to find a new group of friends. Providentially he met a girl who was from another small town where he knew no one. They began to date and she invited him to a teenage club activity. That night he heard the gospel for the first time—though he would tell you his mother had told him the message many times before.

This event led to a whole new circle of friends. From the leader of this group he learned how to walk the Christian life, but he quickly became aware that this new walk was a battleground. There was so much to change. His dirty mouth plagued him. His sexual desires were as strong as ever. His English skills needed significant improvement, and he also needed to learn the vocabulary of Christianity.

During these challenges, his youth leader pointed him to today's focal passage and taught him how to be alert, how to stand firm, and how to choose to be a strong Christian man. He reports that his life was transformed through empowerment of the indwelling Christ. Worshiping, studying the Scripture, and resisting temptation all became a way of life into which he integrated sports, education, and work.

My troubled friend graduated from the university where he met his wife, pursued graduate school, and became a godly husband and father as well as a leader in Christ's church.

Of course, there are many truths to grasp that are important to living the Christian life, but those packaged in this verse are vital for avoiding the schemes of the devil, and thus effectively capitalizing on the new beginning experienced in coming to Christ. So, let's ask, "How do you need to implement these truths in your life today?"[17]

Prayer

Lord Jesus, You not only died to save me from my past sin, but to save me from the power of sin. You have freed me from slavery to sin to give me a new beginning. By Your Spirit You indwell and empower me to choose not to sin. Through the Apostle Paul in this

---

[17] Dr. William Hines made an observation with which we concur. He wrote, "Colossians 1:21-23 can be interpreted to mean that Christians will have a good presentation to the Lord at the Judgment Seat of Christ if they continue in the faith (my preference). Others interpret these verses to mean that people are reconciled to God in salvation if they continue or adhere to the Christian faith."

passage You have taught me to be alert to temptation. Thank You for the continual instruction in how to walk in obedience. Amen.

Interact with Biblical Truths (COMPLETE AT LEAST ONE EACH DAY)

➢ For each of the things this youth leader taught the young man, explain how you do each thing. For the ones you do not do, write a plan for how to begin doing each thing.

How I do what the youth leader taught / My plan to begin doing each thing
To be alert
To stand firm
To choose to be a strong Christian man or woman

➢ For each of the things this youth leader taught the young man, explain how you would teach each one to a new Christ-follower.

How I would teach a new Christ-follower
To be alert

How I would teach a new Christ-follower
To stand firm
To choose to be a strong Christian man or woman

> Make a list of at least three people you know (new Christ-followers, children, youth, adults) with whom you need to share. Which of the things the youth leader taught do you need to share with each person?

Person	Truth I need to share

Notes, Thoughts, and Questions

_____

_____

_____

_____

Satan, like a good chess player,

is always trying to maneuver you into

a position where you can save your castle,

only by losing your bishop."

~C. S. Lewis~
Irish Author, Christian Apologist

Devo 21

Howard

A man after God's own heart
READ: Acts 13:16-25

Scripture Observations

_____

_____

_____

_____

After removing Saul, he made David their king.
God testified concerning him:
'I HAVE FOUND DAVID SON OF JESSE,
A MAN AFTER MY OWN HEART;
HE WILL DO EVERYTHING I WANT HIM TO DO.'"
Acts 13:22

Contemplate the Devotion

Would the Lord write this epitaph for you?

What were the parameters in the life of young David, the shepherd boy who became king of Israel, that he was awarded this badge of distinction from the Lord: *"A man after my own heart"*? I would suggest three.

Humility: Numerous verses from his psalms could be cited, but Psalm 9:1 (NASB) catches the flavor. He does not take the credit for all he accomplished. Instead, he says, *I will praise you, O Lord, with all my heart; I will tell of all your wonders.* There were

137

times when he acted proudly. One example was his taking a census of the people (2 Samuel 24:1-25). But, pride was not his character.

Repentance: David committed such horrendous sins as stealing another man's wife (a respected friend and faithful servant, at that), manipulation to cover his sin, and then conspiracy leading to murder. His resistance to conviction of sin and the toll on his soul is recorded in Psalms 32 and 38. He finally broke when Nathan the prophet confronted him. He could have had Nathan executed, but he did not. His repentance recorded in Psalm 51 has become a model of repentant prayer. Yes, God had to break him, but he became deeply repentant.

Dependency: Both the history of David's life and the psalms that he penned pour out his heart's witness that he was a man who depended upon the Lord. Was he perfectly dependent? No! But again, it was his character to be dependent.

If you read the commentators, you will find a wide range of suggestions regarding the reasons for God's commendation of David. Early on in our relationship, I had this discussion with my mother-in-law, Betty Clark, a well-read and thoughtful Christian woman. She suggested the traits of repentance and dependency. Out of that discussion I added humility.

These three are certainly parameters within which David lived his life. It is good for us to have personal parameters for our lives. Yes, we all need to be humble, repentant, and dependent upon the Lord. But rather like setting basic life goals, we each need parameters that shape and give motivation and purpose to our individual lives.

Today, give some consideration to the parameters of your life. What are the three or four words or phrases that sum up who and what you are and do?

Prayer

Father, help me discern a few words or phrases that can become the parameters that frame my life. There are so many distractions in this world trying to claim my efforts and passion. Grant that I may latch on to lights in the port of life that line up and guide me homeward to achieve your purposes in my life. In the Name of Jesus, the Light of Life, Amen.

Interact with Biblical Truths (COMPLETE AT LEAST ONE EACH DAY)

➢ Write three or four words or phrases that sum up who and what you are and do.

_____

_____

_____

_____

➢ List parameters you have in place that shape and give motivation and purpose to your life. If you currently have no parameters set, list at least three parameters that you can put into place in your life.

_____

_____

_____

_____

➢ List distractions you face that tend to diffuse your efforts and passion for Christ. Write a parameter to put in place to help guard against succumbing to each distraction.

Distractions	Parameters

Notes, Thoughts, and Questions

_____

_____

_____

_____

Devo 22

Howard

You will receive power
READ: Acts 1:4-8

Scripture Observations

_____

_____

_____

_____

"But you will receive power
when the Holy Spirit comes on you;
and you will be my witnesses in Jerusalem,
and in all Judea and Samaria, and to the ends of the earth."
Acts 1:8

Contemplate the Devotion

Now that was a new beginning, the Spirit of God coming upon the disciples! His coming was all about a new beginning; the beginning of the New Testament church that would be composed of Jews and Gentiles. Gentiles would no longer be proselyted into Judaism. No, both Jew and Gentile would be assimilated into what the Apostle Paul would refer to as the Body of Christ.

Talk about counterculture: there had not been, and would not be again, a sociological phenomenon to compare to this occurrence. It was not that Jews always hated all Gentiles, it was more that Gentiles were considered the scum of the earth; vermin to deal with. They were often referred to as dogs. Remember how the woman at the well was surprised that Jesus would ask her, a woman and worse yet, a Samaritan woman, for a drink of water (John 4:4-25)?

But now the Holy Spirit was coming upon the disciples (the church). Everything was going to be different. Impetuous, prideful Peter would become the featured speaker at Pentecost. He would be the Jewish designee to have the vision on Simon's roof of unclean animals with God saying to him, *"What God has cleansed, no longer consider unholy"* (Acts 10:15 NASB). Immediately following this, he was summoned to the home of Cornelius, a Gentile. Upon arriving he announced, *"I most certainly understand now that God is not one to show partiality, but in every nation that man who fears Him and does what is right, is welcome to Him"* (Acts 9:10-35 NASB).

With God demonstrating that the impossible new beginning is possible, can we ever conclude that there is a situation that cannot have a new beginning when the Holy Spirit gets involved? Let's think of some new beginnings to encourage us to believe that new beginnings can occur in our lives.

First, think of Moses, the murderer, being called to lead the people out of slavery in Egypt. Second, think of King David, the wife stealer, the conspirator, and murderer who authored numerous psalms. Third, consider the new beginning of Saul, to be Paul the apostle. There are many other examples in history, like Saint Augustine and Chuck Colson.

In fact, if you are reading this, it is likely you are a Christ-follower and have experienced a new beginning. The Holy Spirit descended upon you first to call you to the Father and then to take up residence within you at the point of regeneration. So, my friend, rejoice in your new beginning. If by chance you have drifted into a sinful pattern of life, then confess your sins, repent by turning from them, and watch the Holy Spirit lead you into a new beginning. Whenever He comes upon you, He comes with the power to enable you to change and engage a new beginning.

Prayer

What a glorious truth, O Father. That same Holy Spirit that moved over the face of the deep in creation as part of your creative wonder, moves over people to transform them as He did the earth that was without form and was void. Thank you for sending Him in Jesus' place to empower your people. Lord today, help me be sensitive to where the Spirit is moving in my life and to respond in obedience to follow Him even as Peter did when he went to the Gentile home. Amen.

Interact with Biblical Truths (COMPLETE AT LEAST ONE EACH DAY)

➢ If you have drifted into a sinful pattern of life, list it on the left. Repent of each sin, then write a plan to walk in the freedom of forgiveness and not turn back to that sinful pattern.

Sinful pattern	My plan

> Write at least two situations or new beginnings you have been reticent to move forward into. What principles from today's Scripture reading would help you to move forward into that situation?

Situation / New Beginning	Biblical Principle

➣ Read Acts 10:15 again. Are there any sinful attitudes you harbor toward specific people or a particular race? Write a plan to overcome your sinful attitudes.

Sinful attitudes	My plan

Notes, Thoughts, and Questions

_____

_____

_____

_____

When Alfred Nobel discovered an
explosive element that was stronger than
anything the world had known at the time,
he asked a friend and Greek scholar for a
word that conveyed the meaning of
explosive power.
The Greek word was *dunamis*
and Nobel named his invention "dynamite."

~Greg Laurie~
"The Explosive Power of Pentecost"
Jesus.org

Devo 23

Howard

That the next generation might know
READ: Deuteronomy 6:1-9

Scripture Observations

_____

_____

_____

_____

> *He established a testimony ...*
> *he commanded our fathers to teach to their children,*
> *that the next generation might know them*
> *... so that they should set their hope in God*
> *and not forget the works of God.*
> Psalm 78:5-8 (ESV)

Contemplate the Devotion

Today's reading lays out God's plan for Israel to transfer the faith from one generation to the next. Note that it is not a corporate plan at the fundamental level. It is a family plan. It starts with parents being sure that they know God's commandments, statutes, and judgments, which the Lord taught them through Moses. What this refers to contextually is the five books of Moses (Genesis through Deuteronomy).

Secondly, the plan calls for parents to live what they teach: *You should listen and be careful to do it* (Deuteronomy 6:3 NASB). Moses then briefly outlines what this looks like in verses four through six. It is believing that the LORD is God. It is loving Him with your whole being. It is going about life with a conscious awareness of God (verse 6).

Once parents understand these fundamentals, Moses lays out the third step in the plan. We are to diligently teach this Word of God to our children. He explains what this diligence looks like.

It is to take place around the dinner table, *when you sit in your house*. It is to take place when you are traveling, *when you walk by the way*. It is to take place when you put the children to bed, *when you lie down*. And, finally, when you get up, it is to take place in the manner that you greet the day, *when you rise up*.

However, it is not only verbal instruction. You shall also teach by symbols and art (*frontals on your forehead* and *write them on the doorposts*). These aspects are peculiar specific instructions that had a cultural context. But, by principle for us they convey the idea that we should use art and things like wearing a cross on a chain around the neck as a witness to others.

Moses tells them to know their God and to know the legal requirements of their God for living, and then to diligently pass that knowledge to the next generation. In today's focal passage we learn a little more about this command as we read that we are to pass along the Word of God to our children so that they and generations to come can know the Word and can *set their hope in God and not forget the works of God.* We then learn that it is important to pass along the Word of God to the next generation so that they will not be like their fathers, a stubborn and rebellious generation.

In our daily lives, we are to model for our children how to be obedient to God's Word. As they learn from us, they will know how to walk confidently into new beginnings—or any situations—as they obey God's Word and trust His promises.

It is very evident in this passage that this task is intense, continual, and necessary. Hear Moses, hear God, and God may allow you to see your grandchild living your faith.

Prayer

Heavenly Father, I am so grateful for Your Word and how You help me know the way to make disciple-makers of the next generation. Give me the wisdom and strength to be diligent to obey Your commands and to teach Your Word to the next generation. In the Name of Jesus, Amen.

Interact with Biblical Truths (COMPLETE AT LEAST ONE EACH DAY)

➢ For parents: List some things you did (or are doing) to teach your children to *set their hope in God*. If you did not do well teaching your children, list things that you can do now (even with adult children) to teach them to *set their hope in God*.

_____

_____

_____

_____

➢ For those without children: List names or categories of the next generation whom you are teaching to *set their hope in God*. List some of the things you did (or are doing) to teach the next generation to *set their hope in God*.

Next Generation people/ categories (i.e., nephew)	What you did (are doing) to teach the next generation

➢ As a member of a local church, list at least four ways you can help teach the next generation to *set their hope in God*.

_____

_____

_____

_____

Notes, Thoughts, and Questions

_____

_____

Devo 24

Howard

For such a time as this
READ: Esther 4:10-17

Scripture Observations

_____

_____

_____

_____

And who knows but that you have
come to your royal position for such a time as this?
Esther 4:14b

Contemplate the Devotion

Ah, when you read this passage and recall the account behind it, you tend to think that this has nothing to do with your life. You are never going to be in a place where speaking to the king or the president is going to save a whole nation from likely extinction. You are surely right! When we read this account, we fail to see the application to our own lives.

I had an experience that demonstrates that there are many times in God's providence when we find ourselves in situations where we are there *for such a time as this.*

My wife and I were invited to New Zealand to stand in for a pastor for five weeks while he was in Europe to perform his daughter's wedding. Our responsibilities extended beyond his

151

church to several other churches in the area, as a resource to other pastors.

One week we made a circuit, teaching classes in the evening and spending days with two different pastors in two different cities. At one location, I taught from Romans 6 on five imperatives to Christians based upon their union with Christ.

During the fellowship time that followed, a young husband sat beside me and said, "I heard a preacher on the radio say that if a man looks at pornography he is defrauding his wife, and then he added that there were other ways he can defraud her as well. Is that correct?"

I said, "Yes. For example, some guys spend their evenings playing video games and in the process, defraud their wives of connecting time."

He responded, "That is me and that is really what I wanted to ask."

I was there *for such a time as this*. The Lord had touched this young husband's heart through a preacher on the radio. Then he put me there to confirm and explain the application of the truth he had heard. We had further conversation in which he concluded that this marked a new beginning for their relationship.

Always be on the lookout for where God has placed you *for such a time as this*, and be prepared to step out in faith trusting the Lord to lead and guide you.

Prayer

Father, help me not to miss the significance of the providential opportunities You put before me. Help me be alert and help me speak the truth in love so that another might be refreshed, yes, even find a new beginning in some dimension of life. Amen.

Interact with Biblical Truths (COMPLETE AT LEAST ONE EACH DAY)

➢ Scripture is filled with *for such a time as this* moments. For each of the passages given below, describe the *for such a time as this moment*. How did God prepare the person and how did the person prepare himself or herself for that *such a time as* this moment?

For such a time as this moment	How God prepare the person / How the person prepared
Joshua 2:1-7, 15-16	
John 6:5-14	
Acts 8:26-31	

➣ List at least two situations in your life when you have sensed that you were there for that moment and reason—`. Explain what you did to walk forward into the situation, or, what excuses you used to not walk into the situation.

For such a time as this moment	What you did / What excuse you used

➣ Take a few minutes to trace backward from today and mark the path that led to you being right where you are at this precise moment.

_____

_____

_____

_____

Notes, Thoughts, and Questions

It was Sunday morning and the doctor's young child
was having a screaming meanie fit.
Finally, in frustration he looked at his wife and said,
"Well, we just are not going to get to church this morning!"
Almost immediately the infant became an angel.
They went on to church.
That same morning a nurse in the congregation
promised to leave the service early to meet
her family in the next town for a celebratory lunch.
But, when she looked at the order of the service
she noted that her favorite hymn was to be the closing hymn.
She decided to be late for lunch.

That morning they were both providentially there
for such a time as this—to save the Pastor's life.
On the last sentence of his sermon he dropped
with a cardiac arrested.
The two of them were on him in less than a minute
and used their expertise to save the Pastor's life.

A *for such a time as this* moment

Devo 25

Shirley

Unless someone explains it
READ: Acts 8:26-31

Scripture Observations

_____

_____

_____

_____

> *"Do you understand what you are reading?"*
> *Philip asked. "How can I," he said,*
> *"unless someone explains it to me?"*
> Acts 8:30b-31a

Contemplate the Devotion

In a previous devotion, we looked at Acts 1:8, *"But You will receive power when the Holy Spirit comes on you: and you will be my witnesses in Jerusalem, and in all Judea and Samaria, and to the ends of the earth."* We talked about how the church grew and the gospel was being spread outside of Jerusalem.

Today's reading sets the stage for the gospel going forth *to the ends of the earth.* An angel of the Lord tells Philip to go to a specific road leading from Jerusalem to Gaza. We read that Philip got up and went in obedience to do what he was told to do. Now, don't miss the point that he was not told exactly where he was going and what he was supposed to do when he got there. In submission to God, he got up and went. In the same way, we are to prepare ourselves to serve God and be willing and ready to go wherever He leads us to go.

Next, we read that as he was on his way he met an Ethiopian eunuch who was responsible for the king's treasury—a very important position in the kingdom. *This man had gone to Jerusalem to worship, and on his way home was sitting in his chariot reading the Book of Isaiah the prophet.* The Spirit spoke to Philip and told him to *"Go to that chariot and stay near it."* Without hesitation, Philip not only got up and went—he ran to the chariot.

He heard the Ethiopian reading aloud from the book of Isaiah and asked if he understood what he was reading. The Ethiopian replied, *"How can I, unless someone explains it to me?"*

Then Philip starts with Scripture and shares the Good News of the gospel using that Old Testament passage.

The Ethiopian's question always brings to my mind the Great Commission, found in Matthew 28:18-20. This is a well-known passage to most of us, yet we often don't really understand what it is telling us to do. *Then Jesus came to them and said, "All authority in heaven and on earth has been given to me. Therefore go and make disciples of all nations, baptizing them in the name of the Father and of the Son and of the Holy Spirit, and teaching them to obey everything I have commanded you. And surely I am with you always, to the very end of the age."*

What exactly is this passage saying? First, this is a command of our Lord Jesus, not a suggestion. Do evangelism. Absolutely!

Do missions. Absolutely! Do a special ministry of evangelism or missions locally or globally to make disciple-makers. Absolutely! These verses certainly include the imperative to evangelize our family, community, city, state, and the world. Yet it means so much more.

Jesus wasn't JUST saying evangelize your neighbor or go on a local or global mission trip. He was saying, "As you go about doing the things the Lord has called you to do, in the places He has called you to do them, make disciple-makers." As you go about being a physician, or an electrician, a dad, a teacher, or a homemaker, make disciple-makers. This means we are to evangelize the lost and teach other Christ-followers the Word of God and how to apply that Word in their day-to-day lives.

We are to share with others what we know about God. It doesn't have to be in a formal classroom setting. It can be while we're cooking, or shopping, or exercising. Making disciple-makers is a lifestyle. We are to disciple others, who will in turn disciple others, who will in turn disciple others, and so on. We are to make disciple-makers.

The world around us is filled with people whom God is drawing to Himself. They are asking, "How can I know unless someone explains it to me?" Many of our new beginnings will place us in contact with those who do not know Jesus as their Savior. Are you prepared to share the gospel with those whom the Lord places in your path? To be faithful disciple-makers we start at home and go out from there to our church, work, community, city, state, nation, and the world.

Prayer

Gracious Heavenly Father, forgive me for my lack of enthusiasm to share the gospel with those whom you place in my path. Help me prepare myself to be ready to move forward without hesitation when you call me to share the gospel. Enable me to boldly proclaim the gospel message through everything I say and do. In Jesus' Name, Amen.

Interact with Biblical Truths (COMPLETE AT LEAST ONE EACH DAY)

➤ Make a list of people you know who need to hear the gospel. What is your plan for sharing the gospel with these people?

Who needs to hear the gospel?	My plan to share the gospel

➤ List ways you prepare yourself to be ready to share the gospel when a witnessing opportunity presents itself. If you have not prepared yourself in this way, write a plan for how you will prepare to share the gospel.

I have prepared by	My plan to prepare

➤ Describe a situation when you were obedient to share the gospel with someone whom the Lord placed in your path, or share a time when you were not obedient to do so. What did you share when you were obedient? If you were not obedient, write a plan for how you will be obedient the next time the Lord places someone in your path.

I was obedient to share / I was not obedient to share	In obedience, I shared / My plan to be obedient

Notes, Thoughts, and Questions

_____

_____

_____

_____

Let your light shine
READ: Matthew 5:13-16

Scripture Observations

_____

_____

_____

_____

> *Let your light shine before men in such a way*
> *that they may see your good works,*
> *and glorify your Father who is in heaven.*
> Matthew 5:16 (NASB)

Contemplate the Devotion

A fellow with whom I am acquainted (we will just call him Charlie) grew up in a neighborhood of dysfunctional families. His own family was better than most around him, but there were many deficits in his family as well. His father grew up in what we might call the top of the lowest working class, in an early twentieth century industrial city in the northeast. His parents were occupied with surviving. Charlie would say, "Being of German origin, arduous work was as natural as the show of affection was unnatural." His parents' marriage was an economic partnership salted with occasional necessary sex. Charlie would tell you that he despaired at the thought of marriage.

Then in God's providence he came under the influence of a godly young couple who were in their late twenties. Charlie says, "They were kind, caring, affectionate, and lots of fun to be around and they, like me, were Germans." Over time Charlie came to see the light of the gospel through their lives. God used meeting this couple and seeing their good works to change his life. They glorified their Father with living out the gospel, and in doing so, stimulated a new beginning for Charlie.

In Scripture, the Lord Jesus told the disciples that they would do greater work than He had done. That seems to be a stretch until we realize that the Holy Spirit has used and continues to use multiple believers, Christ-followers, to glorify God all over this planet. As fully man, Jesus was a human being limited to one place at a time. Now by the indwelling Holy Spirit working in our lives, thousands upon thousands are observing the light of Jesus in thousands upon thousands of Christian lives every day.

By loving our neighbor, by caring for the poor, by teaching a Sunday School class, by preaching the gospel, by giving a drink of water in Jesus' Name, by writing books that teach the Word, by counseling others how to live a godly life in an ungodly culture, we let our light shine and we glorify the Father.

Have you ever thought about the impossible task Jesus assigned the disciples? *"Go therefore and make disciples of all the nations, baptizing them in the name of the Father and the Son and the Holy Spirit, teaching them to observe* [do] *all that I command* [good works] *you; and lo, I am with you always, even to the end of the age"* (Matthew 28:18-20). This He spoke to the eleven disciples (verse 16). Eleven very ordinary men, unlettered, with no religious authority on earth, and God told them to take His message to all nations and make disciples.

Just how did they do that? Peruse the book of Acts. They observed, or did, all that He commanded them. They did the good works of obedience as observed in Acts and later in the epistles. And what was the result? The Father was glorified and thousands upon thousands found new beginnings in the joy of salvation.

Would you not like to hear the grandchildren of the Philippian jailer (Acts 16) tell the story of his new beginning along with the change and challenges of living godly lives in the Roman Empire? I sure would!

So, dear reader, live obediently working the good works that Jesus assigned to you (Ephesians 2:10). Like the young couple who became the catalyst of Charlie's new beginning, determine to be God's instrument initiating new beginnings in the lives of those He puts in your way by being His light.

Prayer

Father, Jesus prayed, saying *"I have glorified Thee on the earth, having accomplished the work which Thou has given Me to do"* (John 17:4 KJV) and so He instructs me that my good work is to let my light—the light of the gospel in my life—shine by my good works and thereby glorify You by drawing men unto Yourself. Thank You for the Holy Spirit whom Jesus sent in His place, who empowers me to so live. Lord Jesus, through Your Spirit, help me today to let my light shine. Amen

Interact with Biblical Truths (COMPLETE AT LEAST ONE EACH DAY)

➤ List the people you know who need to see your light shining to bring truth, joy, and good works into their lives. In what areas of their lives can you help them?

People who need to see	Areas they need help

➤ List three ways (your assumptions, fears, lifestyle, attitudes, etc.) that keep your light under a basket.

_____

_____

_____

➤ For each of the ways you listed, what biblical truth can help you put aside each thing and follow Christ's command to let your light shine before men.

_____

_____

_____

Notes, Thoughts, and Questions

_____

_____

_____

_____

We are told to let our light shine,

and if it does,

we won't need to tell anybody it does.

Lighthouses don't fire cannons

to call attention to their shining—

they just shine.

~Dwight L. Moody~
19th Century Evangelist

Devo 27
Shirley

Keep loving one another earnestly
READ: 1 Peter 4:7-11

Scripture Observations

_____

_____

_____

_____

Above all, keep loving one another earnestly,
since love covers a multitude of sins.
1 Peter 4:8

Contemplate the Devotion

Throughout my life, I have been blessed and honored to be the recipient of the precious gift of godly women and men who have poured into my life. I am not speaking of the many tangible (often purple) gifts of various kinds that may have been given me; I am speaking of their freely given, intangible gift of love, expressed in very tangible ways.

The number of women and men is so large that there is not enough space or time to name each one (if I could even recall them all), much less to enumerate how they have blessed my life. Among these women and men are parents, siblings, grandparents, extended family, Nigeria mission aunts, uncles, cousins, and countless other women and men of all ages.

In times of brightness and happiness, as well as in darkness and sadness (Galatians 6:2), these women and men have shown me how to live out the Word of God by walking in faith through the trials of life and by giving of themselves totally and sacrificially. They have loved, served, and cared for me in very practical ways that were undergirded by the love of Christ. We have laughed and played (not always at the most appropriate times), cried tears of joy and sadness, encouraged and admonished each other, as we struggled together in prayer with and for each other. The Holy Spirit used these women and men in my life, as they willingly gave their time to listen to my concerns, discuss and debate theology, encourage me to use the gifts the Lord gave me, and always point me to Christ!

I realize that some Christ-followers have not had godly discipling influences in their lives. As a single woman, my heart breaks for women, particularly single women, who have not had godly male influences, or godly male spiritual authority in their lives.

Since the Lord knows me so intimately—as He does you—He knows it takes many godly women and men to teach, disciple, and shepherd us!

These women and men have shown, and continue to show me that the way is indeed sure in Christ, and they remind me that the most coveted gift we give is the gift of love. May we all remember that the source of our gift of love is THE Gift of God's Love, Jesus.

It is important that we prepare our hearts for our new beginnings by asking the Lord to give us a passion to come alongside another Christ-follower by *loving one another earnestly.* The Great Commission (Matthew 28:18-20) commands that we make disciple-makers. Titus 2 admonishes the older—more spiritually mature—women and men to teach the younger women and men. Jesus set the example. He loved His disciples by discipling them.

Into whose life are you ministering the gospel of Jesus Christ?

Prayer

Heavenly Father, I thank You for those whom You have brought into my life to minister the gospel of Jesus Christ. May I be faithful to minister the gospel of Jesus Christ to those whom You bring across my path. In Jesus' Name, Amen.

Interact with Biblical Truths (COMPLETE AT LEAST ONE EACH DAY)

➢ Write the names of at least four women or men who have ministered the gospel of Jesus Christ into your life. Tell how they have done this.

People who ministered the gospel into my life	How they ministered the gospel into my life

People who ministered the gospel into my life	How they ministered the gospel into my life

➢ List at least three women or men into whose lives you have ministered the gospel of Jesus Christ. If you are not currently being intentional in this way, list at least three women or men into whose lives you can begin ministering the gospel of Jesus Christ.

I am pouring into	I can pour into
	.

➢ For these three women or men, write a plan to begin pouring into the life of each person.

I can pour into	My plan to pour into

I can pour into	My plan to pour into

Notes, Thoughts, and Questions

_____

_____

_____

_____

Christ's grand plan for His Church is for every
member to be a disciple-maker by speaking and living
Gospel truth to one another in love.

~William Hendriksen~
New Testament Scholar

Devo 28
Shirley

He strengthened his hand in God
READ: 1 Samuel 23:14-16

Scripture Observations

_____

_____

_____

_____

Then Jonathan, Saul's son, arose and went to David
in the woods and strengthened his hand in God.
1 Samuel 23:16 (NKJV)

Contemplate the Devotion

I had read this verse many times, but never really understood and experienced what it meant until that spring when my big brother Paul and his son Little Tim were killed in a train accident.

As you can imagine, it was a horrendous time in my family's life. Hundreds of our family and friends gathered around us. A dear friend was at Mom and Dad's when I drove in from Nashville, where I was living at the time. My friend barely left my side for the next three days as she prayed for and with me, read Scripture to and with me, cried with me, watched over me, and anticipated my every need.

Countless others, during critical times in my life and the life of my family, have come to me and *strengthened* [my] *hand in God.*

Today's passage finds David moving from place to place as he tries to stay out of the king of Israel's way. King Saul thought David was a challenge to his throne and wanted to kill him. Since Saul's son Jonathan and David were very close friends, Jonathan set out to find David and *strengthened his hand in God.*

What a beautiful picture of the Body of Christ coming alongside and helping each other stand firm in the midst of trials and struggles and to not succumb to temptation.

Let's take a closer look at this interaction between Jonathan and David. First of all, both men trusted in God. Someone who trusts and follows God knows God and is able to bring encouragement to others by pointing them to God.

As Christ-followers, we need our brothers and sisters in Christ to come alongside us and strengthen our hands in God. If David, whom God called *a man after* [His] *own heart,* needed someone to come alongside him to strengthen his hand in God, no one is so strong that he or she does not also need to be strengthened in God. Yes, from time to time even the most spiritually mature among us need encouragement to continue applying the truth of God's Word to our lives.

We also need to make a conscious effort to strengthen someone's hand in God. Jonathan set out with determination to go find David and encourage him in the Lord. Imagine how different our families and churches would be if we woke up every morning with a purposeful determination to go and strengthen the hands of others in God.

We also see that this type of strengthening points others to Christ for their hope, help, and strength. It is not the type of support that is offered in self-help, therapy, or support groups. The focus here is totally different. The point is that we are to remind each other of our position in Christ and of God's promises we know through His Word. When we are experiencing trials, struggles, and temptations, we need other Christ-followers to come alongside us to point us to Jesus and remind us that He is our source of strength.

Prayer

Gracious Heavenly Father, thank You for the Christ-followers You place in my life who strengthen my hands in You. Please grow the passion inside me to come alongside other Christ-followers and strengthen them in You. In Jesus' Name, Amen.

Interact with Biblical Truths (COMPLETE AT LEAST ONE EACH DAY)

➢ List at least four ways that you can prepare yourself to strengthen someone's hand in God.

_____

_____

_____

_____

➢ Write the names of those who have strengthened your hand in God. In what situation did they strengthen your hand? What did they do to strengthen your hand in God?

Name	Situation	What they did

➢ List at least four people you know whose hand needs to be strengthened in God. Why do they need this strength? Write a plan to do so.

Name	Why they need strength	My plan

Name	Why they need strength	My plan

Notes, Thoughts, and Questions

_____

_____

_____

_____

We went to strengthen the Nigerians' hands in God.
What a gracious gift of the Lord we received when they,
in turn, strengthened our hands.

~Gwen Reece~
Retired Missionary to Nigeria, West Africa

I press on
READ: Philippians 3:10-16

Scripture Observations

_____

_____

_____

_____

But one thing I do:
Forgetting what is behind
and straining toward what is ahead,
I press on toward the goal to win the prize
for which God has called me heavenward in Christ Jesus.
Philippians 3:13b-14 (ESV)

Contemplate the Devotion

In today's passage, the Apostle Paul tells us that while our position as Christ-followers is, by God's grace, secured in Christ, we are not to become complacent with our spiritual life. Paul is saying that in our spiritual lives we need to be growing. We call this growth sanctification—the process by which we become more like Christ. We must remain humbly aware of our sin and be quick to confess and repent so that our growth in Christ is not hindered.

How do we do that? We do one thing. But wait, Paul says one thing then mentions two. Well, not really. The one thing is— we forget the past as we press on into the future.

Now that does not mean that we just ignore the past, acting as if it never happened; it means that we are not to let the past make us victims. We are to process the past through the lens of God's forgiveness, mercy, grace, and love, as we stand firm in our understanding of who we are in Christ.

I often read through my prayer journals, and two things always jump out at me: God's forgiveness, mercy, grace, love, and faithfulness, and the depth and frequency of my own sinful thoughts, attitudes, and actions. It would be very easy to dwell on my own sin and failure and the disappointments that have come my way. However, because I am reminded of God's unchanging and unending grace, mercy, and love that has undergirded, surrounded, and elevated me in each and every situation I encountered, I choose to focus on God's faithfulness to forgive and on His grace that empowers me to live in freedom from the guilt and bondage of my sin. That does not mean that when I am reminded of unconfessed sin that I ignore it. I must be quick to put off sinful behavior and put on godly behavior (Ephesians 4:20-24). I am then propelled and compelled to honor Him more by being obedient to His Word.

As we are *forgetting what is behind* we also *press on toward the goal*. Here we have the picture of undeterred concentration as one pursues a goal or prize. Paul is saying that with every ounce of his being, he will pursue the goal or prize of being like Christ. Do not misunderstand him. Paul is acutely aware that *what we will be*—perfect in Christ—*has not yet been made known*, and, he confidently anticipates that when Christ appears, we will *appear with him in glory* (Colossians 3:3).

The Scottish athlete Eric Liddell, who refused to compete in an Olympic race held on a Sunday, said, "It is that in which you have to strain every muscle and sinew to achieve victory that provides real joy." This is the picture Paul is painting in these verses. We are to use every means available to assist us in pressing on into everything, including a new beginning: reading, studying, memorizing, contemplating, and meditating upon God's Word; and being obedient to live out that Word.

Prayer

Father God, thank You for my salvation that secures my position in Christ. Forgive me for not being obedient to Your Word as I have been deterred often and lack passion to pursue You. I pray that Your Holy Spirit would renew in me a passionate commitment to forget what is behind me as I press on to the goal of Christlikeness. In Jesus' Name, Amen.

Interact with Biblical Truths (COMPLETE AT LEAST ONE EACH DAY)

➤ List at least three goals or prizes you are passionately pursuing.

_____

_____

_____

_____

➢ List at least three things you need to "put off" in order to passionately pursue Christ.

_____

_____

_____

_____

➢ List at least three things you need to "put on" in order to passionately pursue Christ.

_____

_____

_____

_____

Notes, Thoughts, and Questions

_____

_____

_____

_____

The Lord bless you and keep you
READ: Numbers 6:22-27

Scripture Observations

_____

_____

_____

_____

> *The LORD bless you and keep you;*
> *The LORD make His face*
> *shine upon you, and be gracious to you;*
> *The LORD lift up His countenance upon you,*
> *And give you peace.*
> Numbers 6:24 (ESV)

Contemplate the Devotion

Recently some war stories have surfaced that give incredible witness to how, at times, the Lord chooses to bless and keep His people. Here are three stories that will stand your hair on end.

John Ingham reported in the *Sunday Express* on March 29, 2014, the story of Harry Taylor as told by his son Roy Taylor. In 1915, Harry was a dispatch cyclist in the British Army. He was targeted by a German sniper and took a direct hit. However, the bullet lodged in his Bible. The force of the bullet knocked him off his bike, without injury. As if that was not enough blessing, a few weeks later another bullet was deflected by his dog tag. Roy observed, "It was the hand of God. He obviously looked after my father."

The Daily Mail, Monday, August 7, 2017, reported the 1917 story of Private Bush, who took a bullet to his Bible in Ypres, Belgium. The Bible stopped one bullet and another ricocheted off of it and went clean through his collarbone with little damage. The headline noted that Bush's devout Christianity saved his life.

Displayed in the magnificent World War I museum in Wellington, New Zealand, another such story is authenticated. The Bible is on display that saved the life of Private Hone Tahitahi when it stopped a Turkish bullet. The bullet rested on these words from Matthew 14:27; "Take courage! It is I. Don't be afraid."[18]

We can only imagine so, but given the level of commitment shown by these men that they would carry a copy of the Bible with them in the breast pocket of their fighting uniforms, it is likely that a mother or a pastor spoke this very biblical passage to them as they departed for war.

We certainly rejoice with the family members of these men who benefited from God's blessings. What is interesting about these reports is that none of these recipients of the blessing of spared life went on to become special people—not missionaries, not pastors, not college professors. Each finished life in very ordinary positions.

---

[18] The Great War Exhibition, Pukeahu National War Memorial Park, Marion Square, Wellington, New Zealand. See: http://bit.ly/2whr1YF

Here is the lesson for us. God's blessings of His face (countenance) and peace being extended to us are not related to our position or station in life. They are a matter of relationship. He has loved us and given Himself to us, and His blessings are new every day.

Prayer

Lord Jesus, right now there are several people on my heart. I ask You to bless them by enabling them to see Your hand on their lives and engage with You in fellowship. May Your face shine upon each one, smile on them and grant them a special consciousness of Your presence and peace. Thank You for all the times You have blessed me as others have prayed for me. Today, enable me to be faithful. Amen.

Interact with Biblical Truths (COMPLETE AT LEAST ONE EACH DAY)

➢ List the people who are on your heart that you are asking God to bless.

_____

_____

_____

_____

_____

➢ List at least four ways the Lord has blessed you as a result of the prayers of other people.

_____

_____

_____

_____

➢ List ways you have experienced God's blessing of His face (countenance) and peace being extended to you.

_____

_____

_____

_____

_____

Notes, Thoughts, and Questions

_____

_____

_____

_____

God will wipe away every tear

READ: Revelation 21:1-5

Scripture Observations

_____

_____

_____

_____

"And God will wipe away every tear from their eyes;
there shall be no more death, nor sorrow, nor crying.
There shall be no more pain,
for the former things have passed away."
Revelation 21:5 (NKJV)

Contemplate the Devotion

Now here is the new beginning of all new beginnings since the six days of creation. Along the way there have been many new beginnings. There was the rainbow after the Great Flood, indicating that judgment was past. Noah and his family started life in a new and fresh world. Unfortunately, it did not take them long to tarnish the new.

God called Abram out of Ur of the Chaldees and created a new godly line with a new covenant. But again, it did not take long before the line was tarnished. Then came Moses leading the exodus from slavery in Egypt with the Promised Land before them. But before they arrived a generation of people had to die off.

Joshua succeeded Moses and led them in conquest with the promise of victory only to have this new beginning marred by Achan's idolatry and lying. And so it goes, till Jesus appears on the scene. He wins the war. His resurrection declares victory. There is a new beginning—the church, the Body of Christ of which you and I are a part—on the journey toward the day when God will wipe away every tear.

And, so it is with our lives. We are born again and are in the process of being formed more and more into the image of His dear Son (Romans 8:29). Yet we mar this new life and need to turn to the promise of God recorded in 1 John 1:9 (ESV), *If we confess our sins, he is faithful and just to forgive us our sins and to cleanse us from all unrighteousness*, to start fresh again. Yet all of us know it will not be long until we are again in need of refreshing.

But, when the new beginning of Revelation 22 is initiated there will be no more marring! Here is the ultimate blessed hope! We reach forward to invigorate the now. As Paul put it, *Yet this is no cause for shame, because I know whom I have believed, and am convinced that he is able to guard what I have entrusted to him until that day* (2 Timothy 1:12).

So, when we are marred today by our sin, let us remember that a new beginning of sinlessness is coming!

Prayer

Lord Jesus, thank You that You are the river of life flowing from the throne of the Father. Thank You that You will eradicate the curse. Thank You that I will see Your face and reign with You forever. Today, enable me to look through this lens of eternity at my NOW. Amen.

Interact with Biblical Truths (COMPLETE AT LEAST ONE EACH DAY)

➤ List two very difficult situations when you reacted sinfully to the situation. Briefly describe how you reacted sinfully.

Difficult situation	My sinful reaction

➤ Thinking about the situations above, write how viewing each of these situations through the lens of eternity would now produce a different and biblical response.

_____

_____

_____

_____

➤ Reread Revelation 21:1-5. List things in these verses that motivate you to share the gospel with others. Then, list how each thing motivates you to share the gospel.

What motivates me	How it motivates me

Notes, Thoughts, and Questions

Testimony

My family walked through a very difficult time when my young granddaughter was seriously injured in an accident. Following several days in ICU, she died.

In the weeks that followed, I began to second guess how we raised our children and what type of influence I have had on my grandchildren.

My friend Shirley sent "That the next generation may know" devotional to me, saying she hoped to encourage us about the way that we had influenced our children and grandchildren by ensuring they knew the Word of God.

Several days later I sent Shirley an email. Here is a portion of what I sent.

> Thank you for sending the devo to me. As I have struggled with God about my precious grandbaby's death, I realize I have been mad at Him because we did the best we could to teach our children how to live according to the Bible.
>
> In the ending statement it said that if you do this GOD MAY!!! Reading that was like a stab in my heart. God has not promised that we would see our children or grandchildren grow up. I know that. I allowed my pain to overshadow Gods TRUTH. I am thankful the Lord led you to send this to me, and that the Holy Spirit convicted me of my sin as a result of what I read. Praise the Lord!

More Scripture Observations

More Scripture Observations

More Notes, Thoughts, and Questions

More Notes, Thoughts, and Questions

Now What?

We recommend you continue your transformation through the Holy Spirit-inspired Word of God (Romans 12:1-2) by being diligent and consistent in your personal reading, studying, memorizing, contemplating, and meditating upon His Word.

Remember, God calls us to walk in worship every day all day when he said, *"Abide in me!"* (John 15:2). Next, He tells us what that looks like. What He says sounds very much like the psalmist who asks, *O Lord, who may abide in Thy tent?* (15:1). Walking in worship is walking in obedience. Walking in obedience looks like:

- ♦ Honoring God with our lips—praise and give thanks throughout the day.
- ♦ Walking in integrity—agreement of our profession and practice.

We encourage you to do a pre-flight check every morning to be sure your spiritual instruments and systems are properly functioning. A devotional and prayer time is a good pre-flight run check-up.

No man is an island unto himself. God places us in the body of Christ when he saves us. That body is manifested on earth in the local church. You need to place yourself under the teaching of a faithful Pastor and Sunday School/small group leader who is a skillful and gifted teacher.

In addition to choosing one of the recommended devotional books and engaging with it daily, choose a plan from one of the recommended online sites for a systematic reading of God's Word so that you read through the entire Bible.

Keep a journal of your devotional thoughts. I (Howard) use a wide margin Bible and write my thoughts in the margins. In fact, most of my devotionals in this volume are the byproduct of those notes.

On the following page you will find recommended devotional books that will help you continue your study of the Bible. These are followed by recommended sites where you can find Bible reading plans.

Recommended Devotionals

A Shelter in the Time of Storm: Meditations on God and Trouble – Paul David Tripp

Cross Talking: A Daily Gospel for Transforming Addicts – Mark E. Shaw

Delight in the Word, 10th Anniversary Edition: Spiritual Food for Hungry Hearts – Paul Tautges

Glimpses of the Savior:30 Meditations for Thanksgiving, Christmas, and the New Year – Shirley Crowder & Harriet E. Michael

Hearing and Answering God: Praying Psalms 1-75 – Stephen D. Cloud

My Utmost for His Highest – Oswald Chambers

New Morning Mercies: A Daily Gospel Devotional – Paul David Tripp

The Quiet Place: Daily Devotional Readings – Nancy DeMoss Wolgemuth

Through Baca's Valley – J. C. Philpot

Valley of Vision: A Collection of Puritan Prayers – Arthur G. Bennett, ed.

Whiter Than Snow: Meditations on Sin and Mercy – Paul David Tripp

Recommended Bible Reading Plan Sites

Back to the Bible: www.backtothebible.org/bible-reading-plans

Bible Study Tools: www.biblestudytools.com/bible-reading-plan

English Standard Version: www.esv.org/resources/reading-plans

Ligonier Ministries: www.ligonier.org/blog/bible-reading-plans

About the Authors

Dr. Howard Eyrich

Dr. Eyrich, after a long ministerial journey of more than sixty years, retired as Pastor of Counseling Ministries at Briarwood Presbyterian Church, Birmingham, Alabama. Over his career he served several successful youth ministries, as Dean of Men in a Bible College, as a church planter, a senior pastor, a seminary president, and a biblical counseling professor at the graduate and lay levels for more than forty years.

He has served on the boards of the Association of Certified Biblical Counselors, Birmingham Theological Seminary, Trinity Seminary, and the Biblical Counseling Coalition, as well as various Presbytery and Presbyterian Church in America denominational committees.to name the major efforts.

His publishing efforts include two books as solo author, three books with a co-author, and numerous chapters in significant volumes in the biblical counseling field, as well as articles for *The Journal of Biblical Counseling* and several other magazines.

Dr. Eyrich and his wife Pamela have two grown children, eight grandchildren and one great-grandchild. Retirement for him is a time for ministry. He writes, teaches, preaches, and travels for the Kingdom. He also enjoys the hobbies of model railroading, hunting, and shooting.

Shirley Crowder

Shirley Crowder was born in a mission guest house under the shade of a mango tree in Nigeria, West Africa, where her parents served as missionaries. She is passionate about disciple-making, which is conducted in and through a myriad of ministry opportunities that include biblical counseling, teaching Bible studies, and writing.

She is a biblical counselor and co-host of "Think on These Things," a Birmingham, Alabama, radio/TV program for women. Shirley is commissioned by and serves on the national advisory team for The Addiction Connection.

Several of her articles have appeared in "Paper Pulpit" in the Faith section of *The Gadsden Times*. She is also a writer for David C. Cook, Student Life, and Woman's Missionary Union publications. She is published as an author, co-author, and contributing author.

Shirley has spiritual children and grandchildren serving the Lord in various ministry and secular positions throughout the world.

Follow the Authors

Dr. Howard Eyrich

Facebook: facebook.com/howardeyrich

Amazon: http://amzn.to/2wSR9FF

Blog: howardeyrich.com

Shirley Crowder

Facebook: facebook.com/shirleycrowder

Amazon: amazon.com/author/shirleycrowder

Twitter: twitter.com/ShirleyJCrowder

Blog: ThroughtheLensofScripture.com

Also by the Authors

Dr. Howard Eyrich

A Call to Christian Patriotism: A Weekly Devotional Essay Series – Howard A. Eyrich

Christian Decision Making and the Will of God: A Practical Model – Howard Eyrich

Curing the Heart: A Model for Biblical Counseling – Howard Eyrich

Grief: Learning to Live with Loss – Howard Eyrich

Paul the Counselor: Disciple-making as Modeled by the Apostle – edited by Bill Hines & Mark Shaw (Chapters 7 & 12)

The Art of Aging: A Christian Handbook – Howard Eyrich

Three to Get Ready: Premarital Counseling Manual – Howard Eyrich

Totally Sufficient: The Bible and Christian Counseling – Ed Hindson & Howard Eyrich

Shirley Crowder

Glimpses of the Savior: 30 Meditations for Thanksgiving, Christmas, and the New Year – Shirley Crowder & Harriet E. Michael

Paul the Counselor: Disciple-making as Modeled by the Apostle – edited by Bill Hines & Mark Shaw (co-wrote Chapter 11)

Study Guide on Prayer—A Companion to Prayer: It's Not About You – Shirley Crowder

Available on Kindle and in paperback from Amazon and most bookstores by request.

Scripture References

Old Testament

New Testament

Hymn Index

Quote Index

Published by:

Growth Advantage Communications, LLC

3867 James Hill Circle

Hoover, Alabama 35226